Does IT Matter?

Does IT Matter?

Information Technology and the
Corrosion of Competitive Advantage

Nicholas G. Carr

HARVARD BUSINESS SCHOOL PRESS

BOSTON, MASSACHUSETTS

Library of Congress Cataloging-in-Publication Data

Carr, Nicholas G., 1959–
  Does IT matter? : information technology and the corrosion of competi-
tive advantage / Nicholas G. Carr.
    p. cm.
Includes bibliographical references and index.
  ISBN 1-59139-444-9
  1. Information technology. 2. Technological innovations. I. Title.
HD30.2.C362 2004
658.4'062—dc22

                                                        2003025722

To Ann,
and to Nora and Henry

Contents

Preface

The Great Debate

MORE THAN FIFTY YEARS have passed since computers began to be used in business, yet there remains much we don't know about their influence on commerce in general and corporate performance in particular. At a broad level, we can't yet say precisely why computerization had little effect on industrial productivity for four decades and then, in the mid-1990s, suddenly seemed to become the driving force behind a sharp acceleration in U.S. productivity. Nor can we say with certainty why the recent productivity gains have been so unevenly distributed, appearing in certain industries and regions that have invested heavily in information technology but not in others that have also spent great sums on computer hardware and software.

When we look at individual companies, the picture becomes even murkier. Information technology has changed the way companies carry out many important activities, but it has not—at least as yet—led to any alteration in the essential form or size of corporate organizations. It has delivered great benefits to a handful of firms, even propelling a few into positions of industry leadership, but for most businesses it has been a source more of frustration and disappointment than of glory. It has allowed many companies to substantially cut their labor costs and working capital, but it has also led managers to plow cash into risky and misguided initiatives, sometimes with catastrophic results.

Simply put, it remains difficult, if not impossible, to draw any broad conclusions about IT's effect on the competitiveness and profitability of individual businesses. Information technology has become the largest of all corporate capital expenditures—and an intrinsic element of nearly every modern business process—but companies continue to make IT investments in the dark, without a clear conceptual understanding of the ultimate strategic or financial impact. The goal of this book is to help promote such an understanding, to provide business and technology managers, as well as investors and policy makers, with a new perspective on how technology, competition, and profits intersect.

Through an analysis of its unique characteristics, evolving business role, and historical precedents, I will argue that IT's strategic importance is not growing, as many have claimed or assumed, but diminishing. As IT has become more powerful, more standardized, and more affordable, it has been transformed from a proprietary technology that companies can use to gain an edge over their rivals into an infrastructural technology that is shared by all competitors. Information technology has increasingly become, in other words, a simple factor of production—a commodity input that is necessary for competitiveness but insufficient for advantage.

The emergence of a ubiquitous, shared IT infrastructure has, as I will show, many important practical implications, both for how companies manage and invest in technology itself and, more broadly, for how they think about creating and defending competitive advantages. The way executives respond to IT's changing role will influence their companies' fortunes for years to come.

Background and Scope

This book deepens, expands, and extends a point of view that I originally presented in an article in the May 2003 edition of the *Harvard Business Review*. That article, entitled "IT Doesn't Matter," has become a touchstone for a wide and often passionate debate among the suppliers and users of information technology. In dozens of articles published in newspapers, business magazines, and IT journals around the world, my thesis has been discussed and dissected, questioned and critiqued, attacked and defended. Many respected executives, business professors, and journalists have probed the strengths and weaknesses of my argument and offered their own views on IT and its meaning for business. Beyond the intellectual and practical value of the discussion, which is considerable, its very breadth and intensity underscore both the importance of this subject for companies and the profound lack of a common understanding of it.

For me personally, the debate has been at once gratifying and frustrating. It has been gratifying because I feel I have spurred a necessary, constructive, and overdue reconsideration of one of the most important business phenomena of the last half century. A relatively brief piece of business writing rarely engages so many people and brings into the open so many contending perspectives. It has been frustrating because at least a few of the criticisms of my article reflect misinterpretations of it—misinterpretations traceable in some cases to my own lack of clarity in defining the terms and scope of my argument. As I elaborate my thesis in this book, I will address many of the questions that have been raised about my views while also expressing those views with, I hope, more precision and thoroughness. I certainly don't present this volume as the last word in what I'm sure will be a long and fruitful discussion, but I do hope it helps move the debate at least a little nearer to concrete conclusions of practical benefit to managers.

Let me offer at the outset a few important definitions, beginning with the somewhat fuzzy term "information technology" itself. I use "IT" in what I believe is its commonly understood sense today, as denoting all the technology, both hardware and software, used to store, process, and transport information in digital form.[1] It is important to stress that I am talking about the technology itself. The meaning of "IT" does not encompass the information that flows through the technology or the talent of the people using the technology. As several writers correctly pointed out in responding to my *Harvard Business Review* article, information and talent often form the basis of business advantage. That has always been true, and it will continue to be so. Indeed, as the strategic value of the technology fades, the skill with which it is used on a day-to-day basis may well become even more important to a company's success.

Nevertheless, the development of a common and universal IT infrastructure does influence and in some cases constrain the way the underlying technology and the information it carries are used. As I hope to show in the pages that follow, one of the greatest challenges facing today's managers is understanding how the new infrastructure reshapes many operational and strategic decisions. Even commodity inputs can't be taken for granted.

It is also important to make clear that I am talking about the technologies used for managing information inside and between companies in what has come to be called the developed world. I am not talking about the use of IT in the home or its incorporation into consumer products, both of which seem to me areas ripe for rapid innovation as the vast computer, media, and consumer electronics industries converge.[2] And I am not talking about its use in emerging markets, which in general have much less advanced IT infrastructures. The sellers and users of IT in emerging markets can learn a great deal from the experiences of their counterparts in the developed world, as I hope this book will make clear, but they are in different positions and face different challenges.

The Plan of the Book

I open with a brief introductory chapter, "Technological Transformations," that provides an overview of my thesis and underscores the value of examining IT from a strategic perspective. I stress in this chapter what I see as the central—and positive—message of this book: that IT's transformation from a set of proprietary and heterogeneous systems into a shared and standardized infrastructure is a natural, necessary, and healthy process. It is only by becoming an infrastructure—a common resource—that IT can deliver its greatest economic and social benefits.

The second chapter, "Laying Tracks," introduces and explains the critical distinction between proprietary and infrastructural technologies. I describe how the business use of past infrastructural technologies, from railroads to electric power, evolved in a predictable way that foreshadowed what we've seen with IT. In particular, the pioneers of an infrastructural technology often gain lasting advantages in the early stages of its development, but as the infrastructure matures and becomes cheaper, more accessible, and better understood, competitors are able to rapidly copy any valuable new innovation.

In Chapter 3, "An Almost Perfect Commodity," I examine the technical, economic, and competitive characteristics of IT that lend it to particularly rapid commoditization. I address in this chapter two of the most significant criticisms of my argument: first, that I overlook the almost unlimited potential for innovation in software and, second, that I ignore the continuing changes in the way IT assets are organized—in the IT "architecture," as technologists put it. While granting that computer software is more malleable and adaptable than earlier infrastructural technologies, qualities that make it less susceptible to commoditization, I will argue that it exhibits other qualities that push it in the other direction—toward commoditization. And while acknowledging the continued evolution of the IT architecture, I will suggest that at this point most innovations will tend to enhance the reliability and efficiency of the shared infrastructure rather than enable proprietary uses of that infrastructure.

Chapter 4, "Vanishing Advantage," looks at the history of the use of IT by companies, showing how closely it follows the pattern established by earlier infrastructural technologies. Some critics of my thesis have argued that "IT never mattered" as a source of advantage. In this chapter I show, through case studies of several IT pioneers, that information systems and networks actually formed very durable barriers to competition in the past but that those barriers have fallen as IT has advanced. I also introduce the idea of the *technology replication cycle,* a concept crucial to gauging whether a strategic IT investment will ultimately pay off.

Chapter 5, "The Universal Strategy Solvent," steps back from the close examination of IT management to describe how the emergence of a new business infrastructure can change the basis of competition in markets. I discuss the corrosive effects of the IT infrastructure on some traditional forms of competitive advantage and describe how business success increasingly hinges on the simultaneous pursuit of both *sustainable* and *leverageable* advantages. I also explain how companies should take care in balancing the need to share information and processes with partners with the need to maintain their organizational integrity. The IT infrastructure makes specialization and outsourcing easier, but that doesn't mean companies should rush to pursue them.

In Chapter 6, "Managing the Money Pit," I turn to the practical managerial implications of the commoditization of IT. Stressing the importance of controlling cost and risk, I offer four guidelines for IT investment and management: spend less; follow, don't lead; innovate when risks are low; and focus more on vulnerabilities than opportunities. I also provide a number of examples of recent company practices that provide models for action. My intent here is not to provide an IT textbook—others are better qualified than I for that job—but rather to offer a new managerial perspective that will help both business and technology managers make appropriate decisions in the years ahead.

The final chapter, "A Dream of Wonderful Machines," explores the broader consequences of information technology for economies and societies. I describe how our natural enthusiasm for a new technology, with its promise of renewal, can lead us to exaggerate its benefits and overlook its costs, and I examine how this bias has influenced our perceptions of the so-called computer revolution.

Such a discussion is particularly timely today. We are arriving at a turning point in the history of IT in business with the convergence of three important trends that will shape the future. First, companies are reevaluating their approaches to IT investment and management as the economy emerges from the post-Internet-bubble downturn. Second, the technology industry is in the midst of a restructuring, as vendors reshape their competitive strategies in response to shifts in the marketplace. Third, policy makers and economists are assessing the broad impact of computers on industrial performance and productivity, which will lead to crucial government decisions about the development of the IT infrastructure throughout the world. Making the right choices in all these areas requires an open exchange of information and views, and it is in that spirit that I offer this book.

Acknowledgments

Several people helped me in arranging my thoughts and words. At the *Harvard Business Review,* my former colleagues David Champion, Andy O'Connell, Anand Raman, and Tom Stewart provided particularly valuable editorial suggestions while I was writing the article that would grow into this book. Jeff Kehoe, my editor at the Harvard Business School Press, helped focus my mind and my argument. Jeff also arranged for five anonymous reviewers, all experts in the IT field, to critique a draft of the book, and their incisive comments led to refinements in logic and prose throughout. Many other writers on business and technology influenced my thinking and helped shape my argument; I document those influences in the notes and bibliography at the end of the book. Finally, I want to thank the staff at the Gleason Public Library, who handled an oppressive number of interlibrary loan requests with unwavering good cheer.

Does IT Matter?

CHAPTER I

Technological Transformations

The Rise of a New
Business Infrastructure

IN 1969, a young electrical engineer named Ted Hoff had a particularly elegant idea. Hoff had recently joined the Intel Corporation, a fledgling semiconductor company in Santa Clara, California, and had been assigned to a project to produce a set of twelve microchips for a new calculator being developed by the Japanese electronics company Busicom. Each chip would be dedicated to a different function: One would perform the calculations, one would control the keypad, one would display images on the screen, one would handle the printing, and so on. It was a tricky assignment—some of the chips would need to contain as many as five thousand transistors, and all of them would need to fit neatly inside the device—and Hoff feared that the total cost of the chipset would end up exceeding Busicom's budget. So he set aside the client's original plan and took a completely different approach. Instead of trying to pack the calculator with a dozen specialized chips, he decided to create a single general-purpose chip—a central processing unit—that could handle many different functions. Two years later, Hoff's idea came to fruition when Intel unveiled its 4004 semiconductor, the world's first microprocessor.[1]

By providing the brains for a new generation of small, easy-to-program computers, the microprocessor changed the course not only of computing but also of commerce. Although computers had been used in business since 1951—when J. Lyons & Company, a British catering firm that operated a chain of popular tea shops, built and installed a mainframe in its headquarters—their size, complexity, and inflexibility had tended to limit their use to routine, rigidly defined tasks like processing payrolls, tracking inventory, and performing engineering calculations. The programmable microprocessor unleashed the full power of the computer, allowing it to be used by all sorts of people to do all sorts of things in all sorts of companies.

Hoff's invention set off a surge of innovation in business computing. In 1973, Bob Metcalfe created Ethernet, the technical glue for local area networks. In 1975, the first mass-produced personal computer appeared. In 1976, Wang Laboratories introduced its Word Processing system, bringing computers to the desks of office workers. In 1978, the first spreadsheet program, VisiCalc, went on sale, followed the next year by WordStar, the first PC word processor, and by Oracle's first relational database system. In 1982, the introduction of TCP/IP, a set of networking protocols, paved the way for the modern Internet. In 1984 arrived the Macintosh, with its easy-to-use graphical interface, as well as the first desktop laser printer. In 1989, e-mail began to flow over the Internet, and in 1990 the World Wide Web was invented by Tim Berners-Lee. As the 1990s unfolded, corporate Web sites and intranets proliferated, more and more commercial transactions began to be carried out on-line, and software makers created sophisticated new programs for managing everything from the procurement of supplies to the distribution of products to marketing and sales.

Along with the rollback of government restrictions on trade, the proliferation of computer hardware and software has been the major force shaping business over the past forty years. Today, few would dispute that information technology has become the backbone of commerce in the developed world. It underpins the operations of individual companies, ties together far-flung supply chains, and increasingly links businesses with the customers they serve. It permeates manufacturing, wholesaling, retailing, and business services; it's found in executive offices and on factory floors, in R&D labs and in the homes of customers. Hardly a dollar or a euro changes hands anymore without the aid of computer systems.

The Great Mind–Set Shift

As information technology's power and presence have expanded, companies have come to view it as a resource ever more critical to their success. The increasing importance placed on IT can be seen most vividly in corporate spending habits. In 1965, according to data from the U.S. Department of Commerce's Bureau of Economic Analysis, less than 5 percent of the capital expenditures of American companies went to IT. After the widespread adoption of personal computers in the early 1980s, that percentage rose to 15 percent. By the early 1990s, it had reached more than 30 percent, and by the turn of the century it had surpassed 50 percent.[2] Even after the recent slowdown in technology purchases, the average U.S. company still invests as much in IT as in all other capital expenditures combined. Worldwide, businesses spend nearly $1 trillion a year on IT gear, software, and services—more than $2 trillion if telecommunications services are included.[3]

But the veneration of IT goes much deeper than dollars. It is evident as well in the shifting practices and attitudes of senior managers and their advisers. Twenty years ago, most executives looked down on computers as proletarian tools—glorified typewriters and calculators—best relegated to low-level employees like secretaries, analysts, and technicians. When a 1981 advertisement for the Xerox Star office computer pictured a manager actually working on the machine, the image seemed ludicrous. It was the rare executive who would let his fingers touch a keyboard, much less incorporate IT into his strategic thinking.

During the 1990s, however, we saw a sea change in management thinking. As the use of computer networks expanded, culminating in the rise of the Internet, even the seniormost executives began to use computers in their daily work—not having a PC on your desk suddenly marked you as a "dinosaur." They also began to talk routinely about the strategic value of information technology, about how they might use IT to gain a competitive edge, and about the "digitization" of their business models. Most appointed chief information officers to their top management teams, and many hired consulting firms to provide fresh ideas on how to use IT investments to achieve differentiation and advantage. A 1997 survey conducted by the London School of Economics found that the chief executives and directors of large North American and European companies believed that by the end of the decade 60 percent of their IT initiatives would be focused on "achieving competitive edge" rather than just "catching up or staying afloat." "This represents," the study's authors noted, "a complete turnaround from the views expressed in the 80s and early 90s."[4]

The turnaround is summed up neatly by the story of General Electric's Jack Welch, the most acclaimed chief executive of recent times. Welch didn't bother to personally explore the workings of the Internet until 1999, when during a vacation in Mexico his wife sat him down at her laptop and showed him how to send e-mail and use a Web browser. Welch was immediately "hooked," as he would later write in his autobiography, and when he returned to work he brought his newfound enthusiasm with him. Within a year, he had spearheaded a "destroyyourbusiness.com" initiative aimed at overhauling GE's traditional business models, had demanded that the company's top 500 executives find young "Internet mentors" to coach them about new technologies, and had asked Sun Microsystems CEO Scott McNealy to join GE's board as a kind of technology guru for the corporation. "Everyone began to think digitally," Welch recalls. "It was a great mind-set shift for the entire organization."[5]

With the collapse of the Internet bubble, the pendulum began to swing back. Over the last few years, as it has become painfully clear that many of the technology investments of the 1990s, particularly the strategic ones, have gone to waste, business executives have again grown skeptical about IT, casting cold eyes on proposals for grand new technology initiatives. But despite the wariness over aggressive spending in this area, the general sense of IT's strategic importance remains strong in the business world and continues to be heavily promoted by the technology industry as well as many consultants and journalists. The "great mind-set shift" that Welch described continues to influence the way businesses view and use IT.

Indeed, the assumed connection between IT and business strategy has become so ingrained in the language of business that we now take it for granted. "Today," proclaim the authors of an article in the prestigious *MIT Sloan Management Review*, "the explosion of digital information makes available a new array of strategic options, bringing within reach the Holy Grail of differentiation."[6] The Blackstone Technology Group announces that "the implementation of future-focused information technology solutions has become a true source of competitive advantage."[7] The CIO of Cisco Systems says that "IT is becoming a more powerful tool for gaining competitive advantage, not less so."[8] Microsoft claims on its Web site that a new information system at one of its clients "delivers tremendous strategic value."[9]

Behind such rhetoric lies one simple assumption: that as IT's power and ubiquity have increased, so too has its strategic importance. It's a reasonable assumption, even an intuitive one. But it's mistaken. What makes a business resource truly strategic—what gives it the capacity to be the basis for a sustained competitive advantage—is not ubiquity but scarcity. You gain an edge over rivals only by having something or doing something that they can't have or do. By now, the core functions of IT—data storage, data processing, and data transport—have become available and affordable to all. Information technology's very power and presence have begun to transform it from a potentially strategic resource into what economists call a commodity input, a cost of doing business that must be paid by all but provides distinction to none.

The Strategic View

So what? one might ask. Isn't it enough for IT to enable companies to operate more efficiently or deliver better service, to reduce costs or heighten customer satisfaction? What's so important about achieving distinctiveness anyway? The answer is this: Distinctiveness is what in the end determines a company's profitability and assures its survival. If a group of firms competing in a free market are indistinguishable—if their products are made and distributed in the same ways and look the same to customers—then they will have only one basis for competition: pricing. In battling to make a sale, they will continually undercut one other's prices until, with the brutal logic of the marketplace, the prices of their products fall close to the cost of their production. All the companies will be forced to subsist on the slenderest of profit margins, teetering precariously on the dividing line between loss and gain.

If, however, one of the companies is able to set itself apart from the pack—to achieve that "Holy Grail of differentiation"—then it can avoid the ruinous effects of price competition. If it can find a way to make its products more attractive to buyers than competing brands, it can set its price a bit higher and earn a premium on each sale. Or if it can find a way to produce its products more cheaply than its rivals, it can turn a nice profit even at the market's prevailing price point—while its competitors earn little or nothing. The achievement of differentiation is the overriding goal and the final test of every business strategy. In the long run, it's the only way a company can boost its earnings and safeguard its future.

Investments in resources that provide differentiation can, by themselves, deliver attractive returns in the form of higher profits, while investments in resources that are broadly shared—that are commodity inputs—cannot. Any increases in productivity or customer value that commodity resources produce will in time be competed away. The gains will end up in the hands of customers, not on the bottom line. Of course, companies often have no choice but to spend money, sometimes lots of it, on commodity resources. In many cases, they simply couldn't operate without them—think of office supplies or raw materials or electricity. And even if a commodity isn't essential to operations, companies may still have to invest in it simply to stay even with the pack—to block competitors from gaining an advantage. What's crucial is to be able to distinguish commodity resources from resources that do have the potential to create advantage. Only then will a company avoid wasted cash and strategic dead-ends.

Looking Forward, Looking Back

For business executives, the transformation of IT from a source of advantage to a cost of doing business raises a host of challenges. They will need to take a hard look at how much they spend on IT and how they allocate those expenditures. They will need to reevaluate the way they manage their IT assets and staff. And they will need to rethink their relationships with the vendors that supply hardware, software, and related services. Such reassessments will lead different companies to different conclusions, depending on their particular circumstances, strengths, and weaknesses. Most companies, though, will find that as IT merges into the general business infrastructure, mitigating risk becomes more important than pursuing innovation, and reducing costs takes precedence over making new investments. Success, in other words, hinges more on defense than offense.

Any fundamental shift in the business infrastructure also influences the nature of competition among companies. Some traditional advantages become less important or less sustainable, while others gain new or enhanced salience. Beyond IT management itself, therefore, managers are likely to face difficult and complex strategic questions in the months and years ahead. Is our company properly positioned in our industry or do we need to change the role or roles we play? Will competitors find it easier to replicate the capabilities that once distinguished us? Should the size or scope of our organization change? Should we forge new or different relationships with other companies? When the business infrastructure changes, the chances and the costs of strategic missteps grow.

As managers grapple with these operational, organizational, and strategic challenges, they should take particular care to rid themselves of the illusions that new technologies often inspire—and that have been a particular hallmark of what has come to be called the digital age. Although it's increasingly unlikely that IT will give individual businesses an advantage, those executives with the steadiest, least distorted view of IT's changing role will be able to make smarter, sounder choices than their less cold-eyed and clear-headed rivals. And that in itself can be the basis for a strong and durable competitive edge.

When faced with a new and complicated situation, the wise manager always looks backward before moving forward, knowing that even the most disorienting of phenomena usually have precedents in the past. That is certainly the case with the transformation of IT's role. Information technology, in fact, is perhaps best understood as the latest in a series of broadly adopted technologies that have reshaped industry over the past two centuries—from the steam engine and the railroad to the telegraph and the telephone to the electric grid and the highway system. For brief periods, as they were being built into the infrastructure of commerce, all these technologies opened opportunities for smart, forward-looking companies to gain real advantages over their competitors. But as their availability increased and their cost decreased—as they became ubiquitous—they all became commodity inputs. They would often continue for many years to spur broad enhancements in business practices and to lift the productivity of entire industries. But from a strategic standpoint they began to become invisible; they mattered less and less to the competitive fortunes of individual companies.

Information technology is heading down the same path. As it becomes cheaper and more standardized, as its power and capabilities begin to outstrip most companies' needs, the advantages it once provided are dissipating, and its great transformational power is starting to fade. This change, the past makes clear, is both natural and necessary. As was true with railroads and electricity and highways, it is only by becoming a shared and standardized infrastructure that IT will be able to deliver its greatest economic and social benefits, raising productivity and living standards and serving as a platform for a range of new and desirable consumer goods and services. History reveals that IT needs to become ordinary—needs to lose its strategic importance as a differentiator of companies—if it is to fulfill its potential.

CHAPTER 2

Laying Tracks

The Nature and Evolution of
Infrastructural Technologies

MODERN BUSINESS WAS BORN, it might be argued, in the fall of 1829 in the small English village of Rainhill. Situated ten miles east of Liverpool, Rainhill lay directly in the path of the Liverpool and Manchester railroad, a major new line that had been under construction since 1826 and was expected to be completed by the end of 1830. The cost of laying the thirty-two miles of track would come to exceed a half million pounds sterling, making it at the time the most expensive railroad ever built. The owners of the line, eager to recoup their vast investment, were desperate to enhance rail transport's attractiveness by increasing its speed. At the time, trains rarely went more than ten miles an hour, making them little faster than horse-drawn carriages.

Knowing that any meaningful increases in velocity would have to come from technical innovations in the design of locomotives, the railway's owners decided to organize an unusual competition on the outskirts of Rainhill. Five newly designed, state-of-the-art steam locomotives, the Rocket, the Novelty, the Sans Pareil, the Cycloped, and the Perseverance, were to be driven a distance of seventy miles—twenty round-trips over a one-and-three-quarter-mile stretch of track—and the one completing the course with the greatest speed and efficiency was to be awarded a prize of £500. The designer of the winning entry could also anticipate a lucrative contract for supplying the locomotives used on the new line.

The weeklong Rainhill Trials, as they came to be called, attracted spectators from around the country as well as intense coverage by the British press. The competition didn't turn out, however, to be much of a contest—only the Rocket was able to complete the full distance without breaking down. Nevertheless, the event held great historical significance. The engines, outfitted with the latest steam-power technology, achieved unprecedented speeds during their runs, with the Novelty at one point reaching 32 miles an hour and the Rocket able to sustain a speed of 30 miles an hour. The age of high-speed, long-distance transportation had arrived.

The importance of the Rainhill Trials was not lost on those in the audience. A particularly farsighted reporter for the weekly *Mechanics Magazine* wrote expansively about the steam locomotive's revolutionary potential:

*We think we shall not go too far in saying, that it will produce
an entire change in the face of British society. The effect will be
much the same, as if the workshop of the manufacturer were
brought alongside the quay where he obtains his raw material
and whence he sends it forth again in a manufactured shape to
the most distant parts of the world, or as if the collieries, iron
mines, and potteries of the heart of England were scattered along
its shores. Peculiar local advantages will figure less than they
have done in our manufacturing and commercial history, since
whatever one place produces, can [be] as quickly and cheaply
transported to another; and instead of our manufacturers continuing concentrated in two or three large towns—to the great injury
of the moral and physical condition of those employed in them—
we may expect to see them spreading gradually over the whole
kingdom. Living in the country, will no longer be a term synony-
mous with every sort of inconvenience, and it will come to be a
mere matter of choice, whether a man of business lives close by
his counting-house, or thirty miles from it. . . . In proportion, too,
as the intercourse of men with each other, and the interchange of
commodities between them is thus facilitated, the greater will be
the cheapness of everything.*[1]

The anonymous reporter's prophecy turned out to be remarkably accurate. As the nineteenth century proceeded, the
rapid expansion of railroads, in conjunction with the advance
of related technologies like steam power and telegraphy, would
transform commerce almost everywhere in the world. Railroad tracks, and the telegraph wires that ran alongside them,
would become the new infrastructure of business, connecting

across great distances producers of goods with their suppliers and customers. Combined with ongoing developments in ocean and coastal shipping, the spread of railroads brought into being global markets and global competition and, in turn, radically new business organizations and methods.

The rail system was to prove the first of several widely adopted technologies that would connect far-flung companies into an ever more tightly woven network. In addition to the telegraph system, with its intracontinental wires and intercontinental cables, there would be the electric grid, the telephone system, the highway system, radio and television broadcasting, and, in our own time, the computer network. Various contemporary commentators have noted the resemblances among these technologies, and many have identified particularly strong parallels between the rollout of the rail network in the mid-1800s and the expansion of information technology, particularly the Internet, in the late 1900s.[2]

But there's been something missing in those comparisons. Most of them have focused either on the investment pattern associated with the deployment of the technologies—the boom-to-bust cycle, with its attendant investment mania—or on their role in transforming entire industries. Little has been said about the way these technologies have influenced—or failed to influence—competition among individual companies.

Yet it's here, at what economists call the "firm level," that history offers some of its most profound lessons. The story of the railroads, and of the other great industrial technologies of the nineteenth and early twentieth centuries, presents us with a pattern of how businesses adapt to broad technological changes and how the process of adaptation influences competition and strategy. And when we step back a bit from the technological tumult of the last thirty years, we find that it's a pattern that closely matches what we've seen as companies have rushed to incorporate ever more powerful and sophisticated information technologies into their businesses.

Advantages of Access

It's important at the outset to draw a distinction between *proprietary technologies* and what might be called *infrastructural technologies*. Proprietary technologies can be owned, actually or effectively, by a single company. A pharmaceutical firm, for example, may hold a patent on a particular compound that serves as the basis for a family of drugs. An industrial manufacturer may discover an innovative way to employ a process technology that competitors find hard to replicate. A consumer goods company may license exclusive rights to a new packaging material that gives its product a longer shelf life than other brands. As long as they remain protected from competitors, proprietary technologies can be the basis for long-term strategic advantages, enabling companies to reap higher profits than their rivals.

Infrastructural technologies, in contrast, offer far more value when shared than when used in isolation. Think back, for a moment, to the days of the Rainhill Trials, and imagine that one manufacturing company held ownership rights over all the technology required to create a railroad—the tracks and the switches, the locomotives and the railcars. If it wanted to, that company could just build proprietary lines between its suppliers, its factories, and its distributors and run its own trains on the tracks. And it might well operate more efficiently as a result. But, for the broader economy, the value produced by such an arrangement would be trivial in comparison with the value that would be produced by building an open rail network connecting many companies and many buyers. The characteristics and economics of infrastructural technologies, whether railroads or telegraph lines, electric power plants or highways, make it inevitable that they be broadly shared—that they become part of the general business infrastructure.

At times, however, the distinction between infrastructural and proprietary technologies can blur. In the early phases of its development, an infrastructural technology can, and often does, take the form of a proprietary technology. As long as access to the technology is restricted—through physical limitations, high costs, government regulations, or a lack of usage standards—individual companies often have opportunities to use it to gain advantages over rivals.

That was true of railroads during much of the nineteenth century, when lines were unevenly distributed and such critical variables as track gauges, coupling designs, and even time zones had yet to be standardized. Manufacturers with easy access to rail transport, and in particular to long lines with many branches, could achieve a level of efficiency in bringing in raw materials and shipping out finished goods that more isolated competitors couldn't match. The opening of the Baltimore and Ohio Railroad in 1830, for instance, proved a boon for businesses located near Baltimore, eventually giving them superior connections both to the coal mines of the mid-Atlantic and to new Western markets. Even as the railroads expanded and integrated, having better access to the system continued to deliver advantages, as some forward-thinking companies realized. Between 1882 and 1884, two Chicago meatpackers, Armour and Swift, aggressively constructed new facilities near key rail locations, establishing the foundations for a national distribution network. The moves helped them rise to dominant positions in the industry, which they were able to defend for many years.[3]

Access to the telegraph system also provided nineteenth-century merchants and manufacturers with great advantages. Companies engaged in national or international trade, for instance, could use the telegraph to gain daily or even hourly updates on shifts in prices and demand, while those without nearby telegraph stations often had to wait weeks or even months for similar information. Suppliers of industrial goods with telegraph access also benefited: They were able to drastically reduce their levels of inventory as the ordering of supplies became much more efficient and reliable.

In *The Victorian Internet,* his history of the telegraph, Tom Standage quotes from an 1847 article in the *St. Louis Republican* that explained the new technology's dramatic effect on competitiveness: "Commerce, wherever [telegraph] lines exist, is carried on by means of it, and it is impossible, in the nature of things, that St. Louis merchants and businessmen can compete with those of other cities if they are without it. Steam is one means of commerce; the telegraph now is another, and a man may as well attempt to carry on successful trade by means of the flatboat and keel against a steamboat, as to transact business by the use of the mails against the telegraph."[4]

Electric power, another infrastructural technology that emerged in the nineteenth century, provided substantial access advantages as well. Between the construction of the first electric power stations, around 1880, and the wiring of the national electric grid early in the twentieth century, electricity remained a scarce resource, and those manufacturers and other companies able to tap into it—by building their own generators or locating their plants near generating stations—often gained an important operating edge. They could illuminate their workplaces more fully and run their machinery longer and more reliably than competitors who had to continue to rely on more primitive sources of power and light. It hardly seems a coincidence that the largest U.S. manufacturer of nuts and bolts at the turn of the century, Plumb, Burdict, and Barnard, located its factory near Niagara Falls in New York, the site of one of the earliest large-scale hydroelectric power plants.[5]

There are often economic as well as physical barriers to accessing new infrastructural technologies. The costs of rail transport, telegraph service, and electricity were all high during the early stages of their development, effectively locking out many small companies that lacked large pools of capital. Cost barriers are often heightened by other, related investment requirements. To fully use electric power, for example, existing factories had to be retrofitted with wires and electric motors. Even if they could tap into local generators, many companies simply couldn't afford to undertake the necessary plant renovations.[6]

Advantages of Foresight

In addition to gaining advantages through better access to a new infrastructural technology, companies can also steal a march on their rivals by having superior foresight about the best use of the technology. When a technology is in its infancy, information on its application tends to be sketchy and diffuse. "Best practices" have yet to be documented or otherwise disseminated. Companies have no choice but to experiment, learning as they go, and those that pioneer the most effective applications reap important rewards, at least for as long as they're able to keep their practices secret.

The introduction of electric power again provides a good example. Up until the last decade of the nineteenth century, most manufacturers relied on water or steam power to operate their machinery. These kinds of power came from a single, fixed source—a waterwheel at the side of a mill, for instance, or a steam engine next to a factory—and required an elaborate system of pulleys, gears, shafts, and leather belts to distribute it to individual workstations throughout the plant. When electrical generators first became available, many manufacturers simply adopted them as a replacement single-point source, using electricity to power the existing drive system. In the mid-1890s, for example, the Ponemah textile mill in Connecticut stopped using steam and water as the sources of its power and instead ran a cable to a new hydroelectric dam at a nearby river. But it made no changes to its machinery or its operating practices.[7]

What Ponemah and other such companies overlooked was the fact that electric power is easily distributable–it can be brought directly to workstations. Each individual machine can be given its own power source through what's called a unit-drive, or individual-drive, system. Unit-drive systems provided at least three important benefits over single-point systems. They reduced power consumption by obviating the need for a heavy, constantly turning main shaft and alleviating the wasteful friction inherent in a belt system. They took up much less space, allowing for more flexible and efficient factory layouts and work flows. And they increased factory uptime and productivity; if one machine broke down, you didn't have to shut down the whole system to fix it, as you had to with a single-point system.[8]

Smart manufacturers, such as the Columbia Cotton Mills in South Carolina and the Keating Wheel Company in Connecticut, were quick to appreciate these benefits. By wiring their plants and installing electric motors in their machines, they were able to dispense with their cumbersome, inflexible, and costly shaft-and-belt systems, and they thus gained important advantages over their less insightful counterparts. In a speech in 1901, Columbia University Professor F. B. Crocker, an early expert in electric-drive manufacturing, reported on the gains being reaped by early adopters: "It is found that the output of manufacturing establishments is materially increased in most cases by the use of electric driving. It is often found that this gain actually amounts to 20 to 30 percent or even more, with the same floor space, machinery, and number of workmen. . . . In many cases the output is raised and at the same time the labor item is reduced."[9]

Around the turn of the century, the construction of central power stations in cities brought the operating benefits of electric power to small, urban manufacturers such as apparel makers and printers. Many of these companies couldn't afford to build their own on-site generators or run lines to hydroelectric plants, but they could afford to purchase power in small quantities from a utility. Once again, those that had the foresight to embrace electric power and restructure their machinery and operating practices gained an important competitive edge, one that sometimes lasted many years. As Amy Friedlander notes in her book *Power and Light,* "it was quite some time before the advantages of restructuring were widely appreciated."[10]

In addition to enabling new, more efficient operating methods, infrastructural technologies often bring broader changes in markets, as the reporter for *Mechanics Magazine* understood. The precise characteristics of the ultimate end-state are always unclear as the technology is being rolled out, and this provides another opportunity for gaining advantage through superior foresight. Those companies best able to anticipate how the technology will change business can establish an edge over their more myopic competitors. In the mid-1800s, when rail lines began to be laid in earnest, it was already possible to transport goods over long distances—hundreds of steamships plied the rivers of the world, and thousands of horse-drawn carriages rolled along earthen or wooden turnpikes. Many businessmen no doubt assumed that rail transport would essentially build on the existing transport model, with various small improvements.

In fact, the greater speed, capacity, and coverage of the railroads fundamentally changed business. It suddenly became economical to ship finished products, rather than just raw materials and industrial components, over long distances, and the mass consumer market came into being. Companies that were quick to recognize the broader opportunity reaped strong, often overwhelming, advantages. Retailing, for instance, was almost entirely a local business up until 1850. The small merchants scattered throughout towns and cities couldn't even afford to take title to the goods they sold. Instead, they worked on commission, relying on manufacturers to shoulder all the transport fees and inventory holding costs. By dramatically reducing the time and risk of long-distance shipments, the railroads changed the economics of retailing. It became feasible for one company to offer a much broader array of goods to a much more diverse set of customers. The merchants who were first to understand this shift and change their business practices to take advantage of it—taking ownership of the products they sold, for instance, and making money on markups rather than commissions—achieved enormous advantages over the traditional, small-scale sellers. It was at this time that such dominant retailers as Macy's, Woolworth, and Sears, Roebuck emerged.[11]

A similar, if even more dramatic, transformation came to manufacturing. As in retailing, most goods production up to the mid-1800s was carried out in small-scale, independent plants. It was only when rail and shipping lines made it possible to serve national and even international markets efficiently, and the telegraph made the coordination of far-flung operations possible, that large-scale manufacturing came into being. Once again, the companies that were first to see the emerging change and to build mass-production factories, or networks of factories, gained a huge advantage. In the 1870s and 1880s, pioneering high-volume manufacturers like James B. Duke (later renamed American Tobacco) in cigarettes, Diamond in matches, Procter & Gamble in soap, Kodak in photographic materials, Pillsbury in flour, and Heinz in canned goods gained dominant positions in their industries, positions they were able to hold for decades.[12]

For a particular example, think of the homely craft of candy-making. Through most of the nineteenth century, making chocolates and other sweets remained very much a local enterprise. Families ran small plants, turning out just enough goods to fulfill the demands of their neighbors. But in the late 1880s, an itinerant confectioner named Milton Hershey began to see something that other small candy-makers did not: The new transport and communications infrastructure was opening up a vast market for mass-produced goods, including candy. Soon, Hershey had built his small family firm, the Lancaster Caramel Company, into the nation's largest caramel manufacturer. He then sold that company and used the proceeds to launch another, much more ambitious enterprise: the Hershey Chocolate Company.

Hershey designed his eponymous company with the mass market firmly in mind, relying on the now-maturing rail network and telegraph system to connect his increasingly widespread operations. In Cuba, Hershey even built his own railroad, laying tracks to connect his two Cuban sugar mills with the vast sugar-cane plantation he owned on the island. To promote his products, he advertised widely in the many national and regional newspapers and magazines that had sprung up after the new transport infrastructure provided an efficient means of broad distribution. As Hershey's empire expanded, the revenues and profits he took in dwarfed those of the traditional, small-scale candy-makers. With his large-scale production methods and his coast-to-coast distribution network, he succeeded in turning chocolate from an exotic luxury good into a cheap treat for the masses.[13]

Building the Infrastructure

The success of companies like Hershey, Macy's, and Armour does not go unnoticed, of course. Their outsized revenues and earnings draw increasing attention to the transformational potential of infrastructural technologies. Other business owners and managers, seeing the great gains—in operating efficiency, customer satisfaction, market reach, and, most important, profitability—being reaped by their early-moving counterparts, soon follow in their tracks, looking to share in the success (or at least prevent their own obsolescence).

The broadening embrace of a new infrastructural technology and its most efficient modes of application is both natural and necessary. Rampant copycat-ism is how the beneficial effects of technologies diffuse throughout an economy. The trap that executives often fall into, however, is to assume that opportunities for achieving advantage from an infrastructural technology will continue to be available indefinitely. In actuality, the window for gaining an edge is open only briefly. When the technology's commercial potential begins to be broadly appreciated, huge amounts of cash are inevitably invested in it, and its buildout proceeds with extreme speed. Railroad tracks, telegraph wires, power lines—all were laid or strung in a frenzy of activity.

Indeed, one of the great story lines of the nineteenth and early twentieth centuries is the massive, explosive buildout of the great infrastructural technologies of the Second Industrial Revolution. In the thirty years between 1846 and 1876, the world's rail trackage increased from 17,424 kilometers to 309,641 kilometers while steamship tonnage grew from 139,973 to 3,293,072 tons.[14] The telegraph system had an even swifter buildout. In continental Europe, there were just 2,000 miles of telegraph wire in 1849; twenty years later, there were 110,000.[15] In the United States, there was a single forty-mile-long telegraph line in 1846. By 1850, more than twelve thousand miles of wire had been strung. Two years later, the network had nearly doubled again, to twenty-three thousand miles.[16] The pattern continued with electric power and the telephone. The number of central stations operated by utilities grew from 468 in 1889 to 4,364 in 1917, and the average capacity of each increased tenfold, from 256 to 2,763 horsepower.[17] The number of telephones in the Bell system multiplied from eleven thousand in 1878 to 800,000 in 1900 to 15 million in 1930.[18]

By the end of the rapid buildout phase, the opportunities for companies to use an infrastructural technology for individual advantage have diminished greatly. As the physical barriers to its use are removed, the technology becomes widely accessible. At the same time, it becomes broadly affordable as the rush to invest leads to more competition, greater capacity, further technological advances, and rapid price declines. The price to send a ten-word telegraph message, for example, fell from $1.55 in 1850 to $1.00 in 1870 to 40 cents in 1890.[19] Electricity rates plummeted even faster, with the average cost of a kilowatt-hour dropping from 10 cents in 1897 to 2.5 cents in 1909.[20] And because the buildout forces users to adopt universal technical standards—or risk losing access to the infrastructure entirely—the ability of one company to maintain proprietary control over the technology evaporates. Many of the early movers in electrifying manufacturing, for instance, had to abandon their on-site generators and once again revamp their physical plant in order to tap into the cheaper and more reliable electric grid. What they had once produced for themselves they began to purchase as a generic utility.

As the technology matures, moreover, the way it is used begins to become standardized as well—best practices come to be widely understood and emulated. Journals devoted to the technology begin to be published, providing in-depth technical information on its use. Professional societies are formed, allowing engineers and technicians from many different companies to share their experiences and know-how. Consultants and contractors carry ideas from client to client. And the companies selling the technology or related components—

railroads, electric utilities, and the manufacturers of electric motors, for instance—launch advertising and promotional campaigns to educate would-be customers. Sometimes, the best practices end up being built into the infrastructure itself. After electrification, for example, all new factories were constructed with many distributed power outlets; a manufacturer had no choice but to use an efficient unit-drive system.

As knowledge about a technology spreads and its effects on the structure of an industry or economy become plain to see, the advantages of foresight diminish along with the advantages of access. Both the technology and its modes of use become standardized. Although useful innovations continue to be made, they tend to be rapidly incorporated into the general infrastructure and hence shared by all users. The only meaningful advantage most companies can hope to gain from an infrastructural technology after its buildout is a cost advantage—and even that tends to be very hard to sustain as rivals, or technology suppliers, rush to imitate any and all innovations.

In the end, infrastructural technologies begin to fade into the background of business. They often continue to play an essential role in operations and to account for considerable corporate spending for a long time, but they slowly cease to be a concern of a company's senior decision makers. They fall off the management agenda. Just think of the rapid shift in the way businesses viewed electricity a hundred years ago. Early in the twentieth century, many large companies created the new management post of "vice president of electricity," an acknowledgement of electrification's transformative role in companies and industries.[21] But within a few years, as electricity's strategic importance diminished, vice presidents of electricity quietly disappeared from the corporate hierarchy. Their work was complete.

This is not to say that infrastructural technologies don't continue to influence competition. They do, but their influence tends to be felt at a higher economic level, not at the level of the individual company. If a particular country, for instance, lags in installing the technology—whether it's a rail network, a power grid, or a communication infrastructure—its domestic industries may suffer heavily. Similarly, if an industry lags in harnessing the power of the technology, it can be vulnerable to displacement. And new technologies often have long-lasting macroeconomic effects that influence the profitability of all companies.

As always, a company's fate is tied to broader forces affecting its region, its industry, and the overall economy. No company is an island. The point, however, is that an infrastructural technology's potential for differentiating one company from the pack—its strategic potential—inexorably declines as it becomes accessible and affordable to all. Infrastructural technologies provide smart companies with opportunities to break away from competitors, but they do so only briefly.

CHAPTER 3

An Almost Perfect Commodity

*The Fate of Computer
Hardware and Software*

IS INFORMATION TECHNOLOGY an infrastructural technology? Is its potential for providing competitive advantage fading as it becomes more powerful, more affordable, and more standardized and as its implications for business practice and industry structure become more evident and better understood? Is it, in short, fated to become a commodity input like rail transport, telephone service, and electricity?[1]

Such questions are critically important to business managers, but they're not easy to answer. Information technology would appear to differ from earlier infrastructural technologies in a fundamental way: It takes both a physical form, as hardware, and an abstract form, as software. While it's true that prior infrastructural technologies required some "software" in order to operate—trains, for instance, had to have schedules, bills of lading, fee structures, and procedure manuals—none of them could be programmed the way the modern computer can. Once constructed, most of the earlier infrastructural systems were inflexible, providing a single or a few functions. Information systems, in contrast, can be instructed, through software code, to serve an ever expanding array of uses. Any assessment of whether IT is becoming a commodity input must therefore examine it as both hardware and software.

In its physical manifestation, IT certainly shares many similarities with earlier telegraph and telephone networks and even rail and road systems. On the so-called information highway, widely distributed data depots and processing centers—PCs, servers, mainframes, storage systems, and other devices—are connected through a dense network of cables and switches. At this level, IT can be thought of as a transport system, carrying digital data just as railroads carry goods and the electric grid carries energy.

Because they need to be shared, all widely used transport systems are subject to rapid standardization, which by definition erases distinctions between equipment. Rail lines and railcars became increasingly indistinguishable as standards for track gauge, rail and wheel shape, and coupling mechanisms took hold; in time, shippers became oblivious to which rail company owned the particular lines their goods traveled over or the particular cars that carried them. Similarly, once electricity providers and users embraced shared standards for current, voltage, and wiring, the differences between generators and cables became invisible. What company today knows the source of every kilowatt it consumes? Efficient transport requires easily interchangeable equipment.

The history of IT has also been one of rapid standardization, as users have sought ever tighter interconnectivity and ever more efficient interoperability. From early mainframe time-sharing systems, which allowed many dispersed users to tap into a central computer's processing power, through local and wide area networks, which allowed companies to connect their own computers into a single system, through electronic data interchange (EDI) systems, which allowed computers at different companies to talk to each other, and on to the Internet, that great network of networks, computer hardware has become steadily more homogenized in order to facilitate higher degrees of sharing.

The Commoditization of Hardware

We can today see that the commoditization of modern computer hardware began at the periphery of what technologists call the "enterprise infrastructure," with the personal computers and related devices used by office workers and other non-technical employees. From there, it has moved steadily inward toward the core of the enterprise infrastructure. This dynamic of commoditization is neatly reflected in the steady expansion of what is arguably the world's most successful computer hardware company, Dell Computer.

Dell is and has always been a commodity supplier. Indeed, the essential genius of its founder and CEO, Michael Dell, is his unsentimental and unshakeable faith in the commoditization of IT. "In the long run," he has said, "all technology tends toward low-cost standards." [2] Dell's first target was the personal computer. Purchased and repurchased in large quantities by corporations, PCs quickly became highly standardized for a few simple reasons. First, they had to be easy for lay users to operate—no company could afford to retrain every new employee in how to use a uniquely configured PC. Second, they had to talk to one another, exchanging files and messages within and between local networks. Third, and closely related to the first two, they increasingly had to run a shared operating system (Microsoft Windows), a shared microprocessor (Intel or Intel-compatible), and a shared set of basic applications (Microsoft Office, most obviously). Fourth, they had to be fairly cheap, so that everybody could have one.

Michael Dell was one of the first to see that business PCs were fated to become indistinguishable "boxes," and he built his company to produce and distribute them quickly and inexpensively, using generic components, keeping investment in R&D and working capital to a minimum, and selling directly to users. Dell's low-cost, functional machines proved alluring to corporate purchasing agents—in the 1990s, the company became the leading supplier of PCs to companies—and all the other major vendors of business PCs were forced to compete on Dell's terms, as commodity producers. In 2001, Michael Capellas, the CEO of one-time industry leader Compaq Computer, put it concisely: "Dell has made this a cost game."[3] Soon thereafter, Compaq would disappear, merging into Hewlett-Packard.

Through the early 1990s, the rest of the enterprise hardware infrastructure—servers, storage systems, and networking gear, in particular—resisted standardization. Because this equipment lay behind the scenes, operated by IT experts, and served more specialized functions, there was far less need to converge on uniform standards. Manufacturers were able to continue using proprietary chips and operating software, locking their customers in and their competitors out. But as the 1990s progressed, and companies found themselves spending ever larger sums on this equipment, the demand for "lower-cost solutions"—cheaper to buy, cheaper to upgrade, and cheaper to maintain—began to grow, creating increasing pressure to standardize. And the growing speed and sophistication of microchips made standardization possible: Designers of cheap commodity chips were quickly erasing the advantages of the in-house technologies of hardware giants like IBM, Sun, and Hewlett-Packard. The rapid spread of the Internet late in the decade further intensified the trend toward standardized, modular, and easily networked equipment.

First to start down the generic route were servers and workstations, the computers that lie one step up from PCs in the hardware hierarchy. In the early 1990s, these were powerful, specialized machines, produced by a handful of vendors, each of which offered its own distinctive technologies. Sun, for instance, built its servers on its Sparc processor and its Unix-based Solaris software. But as processing power continued to mount, these once-mighty machines became less and less distinguishable from their lowly PC cousins. Soon, basic servers were running on Intel chips, using a version of the Windows operating system. Not surprisingly, Dell moved in, quickly becoming the largest supplier of Windows-based servers. The economics of commodity boxes were, again, simply too compelling for server buyers to resist. When the oil giant Amerada Hess, for example, replaced its IBM hardware with a group of Dell workstations, its annual leasing and operating costs dropped from $1.5 million to $300,000.[4]

Today, with processor speeds continuing to advance and the open-source Linux operating system making deep inroads into the server segment, the shift to generic hardware is accelerating. Google, the operator of the leading Internet search engine, provides a clear indication of what's to come. Although it requires massive computing power to catalogue and search billions of Web pages, the company has cobbled together its hardware using off-the-shelf components, outdated microprocessors, and free open-source software.[5] In 2002, Google's CEO, Eric Schmidt, sent shockwaves through the IT industry when he announced that his company had no intention of rushing to buy the new cutting-edge Itanium microprocessor developed by Intel and Hewlett-Packard. In Schmidt's "vision of the future," as the *New York Times* reported, "small and inexpensive processors will act as Lego-style building blocks for a new class of vast data centers, which will increasingly displace the old-style mainframe and server computing of the 1980's and 90's."[6]

Amazon.com, the dominant on-line retailer, has followed Google's lead. In just one year, from 2000 to 2001, it cut its

IT spending by almost 25 percent, in large part by shifting from servers with proprietary chips and operating systems to cheaper Intel-based machines running Linux.[7] Industrial giant General Electric has taken a similar route. By moving many of its corporate applications onto commodity hardware, it has been able to reduce its new systems investments by as much as 40 percent, according to CIO Gary Reiner.[8]

The same trend is unfolding, if a little more slowly, in storage and networking, two other markets that Dell is targeting. Large storage vendors like EMC have until recently been able to maintain their proprietary hardware and software configurations. Indeed, frustrated by the lack of general standards, Dell in 2001 struck a five-year deal to distribute and in some cases manufacture EMC gear. But, as with servers, hardware homogenization is coming to storage. Already, users and vendors are hammering out technical standards that will enable companies to buy storage hardware from different vendors and manage the pieces as a single system. In late 2003, industry leaders EMC and IBM reached an agreement to share details of their storage software in order to ensure greater interoperability of their equipment. And low-cost competitors like Hitachi, the Japanese electronics giant, are gaining market share by offering generic boxes outfitted with open-source software.[9] As competition intensifies and prices fall, more and more companies will come to view storage equipment as a commodity.

Networking is next. Dell has already introduced a line of simple switches, selling them at about one-fifth the price of industry leader Cisco's competing offering. Higher-end

switches and routers remain proprietary, outfitted with sophisticated and closely guarded chips and software. But here,
too, the writing is on the wall. According to a 2003 article in
Business 2.0, "As is happening in storage, the industry's leaders could well be on the verge of losing their proprietary grip
on networking hardware. Intel and Broadcom are building instructions into networking chips that make the equivalent of
years of R&D available to any interested hardware maker." [10]
As the power of IT advances, yesterday's magical machines
become today's cheap boxes.

There's no guarantee, of course, that Dell will come to
dominate all these hardware markets. It faces intense competition, not just from specialized equipment makers like EMC,
Hitachi, and Cisco, but also from giants like IBM, Microsoft,
and Hewlett-Packard. All major IT companies will fight relentlessly to prevent too much control over the infrastructure
from ending up in the hands of any one company. But the
competition itself promises to further speed commoditization. Whether Dell wins or not, the combat will increasingly
be waged on its terms.

One of the best ways to understand how competitive dynamics lead to the commoditization of hardware is through
the idea of "overshooting." Painstakingly documented by Clayton Christensen in his book *The Innovator's Dilemma,* overshooting is the process by which the performance of a technology product comes to exceed the requirements of most of
its users, opening the door for cheaper alternatives. As Christensen explains, "the pace of technological progress in products frequently exceeds the rate of performance improvement

that mainstream customers demand or can absorb. As a consequence, products whose features and functionality closely match market needs today often follow a trajectory of improvement by which they overshoot mainstream market needs tomorrow. And products that seriously underperform today, relative to customer expectations in mainstream markets, may become directly performance-competitive tomorrow." [11]

Overshooting is a common, perhaps even universal, phenomenon in the computer industry, where product performance improves at a relentless pace. Spurred by the need to satisfy their most demanding customers and to protect their highest-margin sales, technology suppliers compete fiercely to advance the state of the art, adding new features and functions to their products in order to stay on the coveted cutting edge. But each new generation of a technology overshoots the needs of some customers, and these buyers often respond by switching to cheaper, more "bare bones" versions from other suppliers.

Eventually, as the technology continues to advance, the performance of the cheaper versions comes to satisfy the needs of most customers, and the basis of competition shifts from specifications to prices. Overshooting explains why Google can forgo the latest Intel chip, why Amerada Hess, Amazon, and GE can make do with less expensive servers, and why Dell can steadily eat away at new hardware markets, turning competition into "a cost game." It explains why Windows can displace specialized operating systems, and why Linux can displace Windows. Many hardware makers are slow to accept the reality of overshooting. They want to believe that the needs of customers and the capabilities of technology will march in lockstep forever. But while computers may be governed by Moore's Law, buyers are not. Sooner or later, most of them become satisfied with what they have—they just don't need another dose of power or a new scoop of features. The commodity machine is good enough.

Carried to its logical conclusion, the trend toward commodity hardware would end with the disappearance, from a user's standpoint, of the individual components of the physical infrastructure. Companies would simply connect to the infrastructure through a cable or antenna, and all the functions their employees require would automatically be delivered to them. IT would become as simple to use as electricity. And that, in fact, is exactly the goal that many IT companies are now trying to accomplish. In "grid computing," as it's called, networked computers don't just exchange files and share discrete applications; they blend together into, effectively, a single machine. All the processors and memory systems are shared, and the computing and storage requirements of individual users are distributed among them in the most efficient manner possible. With grid computing, the network really does become the computer, as a famous Sun Microsystems slogan promised a few years back, and computing becomes a pure utility.[12]

Such a vision will sound utopian to the many business managers who have had to struggle for years with finicky, incompatible hardware, and it's certainly true that many technical barriers would have to be overcome for large-scale grid computing to become a reality. Nevertheless, rudimentary forms are already up and running. More than two million people have donated their personal computers to the SETI project, a quixotic effort to sift through radio signals from outer space in hopes of finding indications of intelligent life. Terabytes of data, collected by the Arecibo telescope in Puerto Rico, are distributed to participants' computers through the Internet and are processed as spare computing cycles become available. Several commercial enterprises as well are experimenting with linking their PCs and other computers into grids in order to more fully use the available processing power.

What's required for grid computing to take hold on a broader scale is a new layer of software for coordinating all the connected pieces of hardware and a simple interface that hides the network's complexities from users, just as the original Macintosh's graphical interface hid the cumbersome workings of the PC. Many of the major IT vendors, including Microsoft, IBM, and Hewlett-Packard, are working feverishly to construct the required software, hoping they'll be able to spur the spread of grid computing and ultimately profit from it. Should they succeed, the perfection of the grid would mark the final step in the commoditization of computer hardware, rendering all equipment indistinguishable to users. The physical IT infrastructure would be complete—and largely invisible.

The Commoditization of Software

But then there's software. Unlike hardware, software appears to have no tangible form, no fixed or stable identity as a "product." Able to be shaped in a theoretically infinite number of ways to fulfill a theoretically infinite number of purposes, it seems as abstract and malleable as thought itself. As *New York Times* writer Steve Lohr puts it in his book *Go To*, "Software is the embodiment of human intelligence."[13] And how in the world could "human intelligence" ever be considered a commodity?

That, anyway, is the common view of software promulgated by many in the IT business. At a general level, it's an accurate view—there are no limits on software innovation. But it distorts the more prosaic reality of how software is actually used in business. For managers and workers, software does not exist as an "idea," or any other kind of abstraction, for that matter. Software programs, particularly application programs, exist as real products purchased with real money by real people looking to achieve real results. And when seen as a product, rather than an abstraction, software is every bit as susceptible to the rules of economics, markets, and competition as even the most common of physical goods. In fact, software's very intangibility imbues it with certain characteristics that, taken together, make it more susceptible to commoditization than many tangible products.

Software programs are, in particular, subject to extremely strong economies of scale. Creating a program is very expensive, requiring highly skilled labor, painstaking planning, rigorous quality assurance, extraordinary coordination, and endless testing. But because there are few physical constraints on the production of a program once it is written, reproducing and distributing it are extraordinarily cheap—nearly free, in many cases. The history of software development can be explained in large part as an ongoing attempt to more fully realize the latent economies of scale, to amortize the high development costs over as many users as possible. While it has often been said that software wants to be free, it would be more accurate to say that software wants to be shared—or, to put it a different way, that it wants be a commodity input.

In the early 1950s, when computers first began to be used in business, companies had no choice but to write their own code. The hardware makers provided little software, and the software industry didn't yet exist. Every company that bought a mainframe had to develop programs for even the most basic of functions, such as converting binary numbers to the decimal system and vice versa. Given the complexity and cost of writing serviceable code, the duplication of effort was enormous—and, it quickly became apparent, unsustainable. IBM, nervous that the costs of software development would deter companies from buying computers, helped organize a user group for the owners of its 700-series mainframes, the dominant business computers of the time. The group, which came to be called, tellingly, SHARE, had one overarching goal: to enable companies to cut their IT costs by exchanging software. In the first year of SHARE's existence, some 300 programs were freely disseminated among its members, saving them an estimated $1.5 million.[14]

SHARE provides an early example of what can now be seen as a defining tenet of business software: Companies will sacrifice distinctiveness if the resulting cost savings are large enough. This kind of trade-off is not unique to software, of course; it's common in business. When a widely used resource is expensive and subject to strong scale economies, cost calculations will often trump strategic ones. What typically happens in such cases is that control over the provision of the resource shifts from the users to a group of outside suppliers. And, true to form, that's what has happened with software.

As programs became steadily more complex, growing from a few thousand lines of code to hundreds of thousands and even millions, sharing through user groups was no longer enough. Most companies simply couldn't afford to maintain the staff required to produce programs in-house. Instead, they began to contract development to specialized software houses, which first emerged in the mid-1950s and then proliferated through the 1960s. The software writers that companies kept on staff began to shift their focus from writing new programs to maintaining, refining, and troubleshooting existing ones.

By centralizing expertise and serving many different clients, the new software houses provided a much better means of capturing the economies of scale inherent in software development. At the same time, their arrival pushed business software further down the path toward commoditization, beginning its transformation from a proprietary resource to a purchased good. Although the contractors created what were called "custom applications" for their clients, there was actually considerably less customization than met the eye. The contractors tended to specialize in particular industries or business processes in order to be able to recycle large portions of their code from assignment to assignment. "As firms picked up more and more contracts in the same application domain," software historian Martin Campbell-Kelly explains, "the knowledge was effectively captured by software tools and code assets that could be endlessly redeployed for different clients."[15] It was only through such reuse that sophisticated programs remained affordable for large numbers of companies—and that the software houses could turn a profit.

When minicomputers and, subsequently, personal computers appeared in the 1970s and 1980s, three things happened that would further transform software development, shifting even more control to vendors. First, businesses could afford to buy many more computers, leading to a manifold increase in the user base and thus providing even greater opportunities for economies of scale in software development. Second, non-technical employees began to interact directly with computers for the first time, dramatically increasing the importance of simplicity and standardization in software design. Third, networking became increasingly important, pushing companies to replace proprietary "closed" applications with shared "open" ones. In response to these developments, software became a packaged good.

The evolution of packaged software bears a striking and not at all coincidental resemblance to the evolution of hardware. The first popular mass-market applications, such as word processing and spreadsheets, tended to be those with the largest and least technically astute customer bases—those used, in other words, by office workers and others at the "periphery" of the enterprise architecture. From there, packaged applications moved steadily "inward" to automate more specialized tasks. Just as the increasing power of microprocessors and the increasing need for interoperability imposed standardization on ever more sophisticated kinds of hardware, so

those same forces led to the homogenization of ever more sophisticated software applications. By the end of the 1980s,
companies weren't just buying word-processing and spreadsheet programs off the shelf. They were buying generic programs for database management, networking, accounting,
billing, factory scheduling, materials management, computer-
aided design and engineering, human resource management,
graphic design, and on and on. It had once been possible, if
costly, to create distinctive programs for all these technical and
business functions. Now, any company could purchase (or at
least license) the same capabilities, often for just a few hundred dollars.

The rise of packaged business software culminated in the
1990s with the introduction of enterprise resource planning
systems. Pioneered by the German firm SAP, ERP packages
promised to solve, and sometimes did solve, one of the most
daunting and expensive problems facing modern companies:
the proliferation of narrow, discrete software applications. As
companies and their various business and staff units automated one function after another, they soon found themselves
managing a baffling array of systems written in different languages, running on different hardware and operating systems,
and incapable of sharing information. The fragmented software not only cost a great deal to maintain and troubleshoot;
it led to a vast amount of redundant work and errors, as the
same data had to be input separately into many different systems in many different formats. And it prevented executives
from gaining a clear view of the entirety of their business—
they could only see bits and pieces.

SAP's software, and the other competing ERP systems that emerged in its wake, treated core management applications—from accounting to human resource management to production planning to pricing and sales—as modules of a single integrated system. All the modules drew from and fed into a single database, alleviating the need for redundant data entry, reducing errors, and enabling managers to get a much more immediate sense of how their business operated as a whole. Although it was possible to tailor some elements of an ERP system to a particular industry's or company's processes, the technical customization was carried out by outside consultants using standardized configuration tools, meaning that any valuable customization could be replicated by other companies. And by the late 1990s, it became apparent that extensive customization was rarely worth the effort anyway. Companies increasingly chose to stick with default configurations, having realized that modifying the complex programs incurred delays and costs without providing meaningful differentiation.[16]

At a functional level, moreover, there was little to distinguish the various vendors' systems. Whether you bought your ERP from SAP or Oracle or PeopleSoft or Baan, you received the same basic functionality as well as the same benefits and problems. The distinctions between the programs continued to evaporate as the vendors rushed to copy one another's features, with each new generation of the software bringing greater homogenization. By 1998, Ray Lane, then the president of Oracle, was confessing that "customers can't find 5 percent difference among SAP, PeopleSoft, and us."[17]

ERP systems, as well as other enterprise systems that automate, for instance, supply chain management and customer relationship management, were extremely complex and costly to write. Even after SAP had developed a mainframe version of its program, it had to spend nearly a billion dollars to create a client-server version.[18] There was no way that individual companies could write the code on their own. Integrated enterprise systems could *only* come from outside vendors able to spread their development costs over many clients. And as large companies lined up at those vendors' doors, commodity software arrived at the very heart of the enterprise. Once again, in the eyes of business executives, the gains in efficiency from shared software overwhelmed the costs of lost distinctiveness.

When the locus of technological innovation shifts from users to vendors, as it has with software, it becomes ever harder for companies to distinguish themselves. The introduction of machine tools in the late nineteenth and early twentieth centuries provides a useful illustration of how this process works. Machine tools serve as a particularly good analogy to computer software for three reasons. First, they are themselves a kind of software—they automate the making of a part or a good by storing information about its shape, size, and process of production. Second, they can be designed for a virtually infinite number of applications, from the rudimentary to the highly complex. Third, they rapidly became ubiquitous in industry—they were so good at boosting productivity that nearly every manufacturer was forced to use them.

The original machine tools were simple jigs, pieces of wood that craftsmen fashioned to guide the cuts of a saw or router. The more talented a craftsman was at thinking up and making jigs, the faster he could work and the better the quality of his products, giving him or his employer an advantage. At the end of the 1800s, however, the introduction of electric power and electric motors gave rise to much more sophisticated machine tools, and a new kind of business—the machine-tool supplier—came into being. By selling their tools to different companies, toolmakers like the Cincinnati Milling Machine Company were able to achieve scale economies and spread their high development costs over many customers. In the first half of the twentieth century, machine tools progressed rapidly through a series of technological advances, from gearing systems to hydraulics to electromechanical controls. Each stage produced more sophisticated tools that improved the precision, speed, and flexibility of industry.

The advances in machine tools dramatically improved manufacturing, boosting productivity and product quality. But because the tools were made by vendors, who naturally sought to maximize their sales by selling to as many manufacturers as possible, the technological advances tended to diffuse quickly throughout the manufacturing sector. The benefits weren't proprietary to any one manufacturer, at least not for long. As a result, improvements in machine tools often strengthened the overall industry without providing any lasting competitive benefits to individual manufacturers.[19] The "vendorization" of software has followed a similar course.

Software's Future

Software production's economies of scale explain the rise of packaged, generic programs supplied by vendors and shared by many companies. But software is also highly susceptible to the overshooting effect, which adds a further push to commoditization. Like hardware makers, software developers are pressured to constantly improve their programs in order to satisfy "power users" and to stay ahead of, or at least even with, competitors. But with software there's an additional force promoting overshooting. Because software isn't a physical good, it doesn't suffer wear and tear as it's used—it never decays. As a result, there's no natural repurchase cycle. The only way to get a customer to buy a program again is to make the program better—to "upgrade" it. Perpetuating the upgrade cycle by constantly advancing the state of the art has been critical to the economics of most makers of packaged software, but it has also hastened overshooting. Microsoft, for example, launched many lucrative upgrades to its Office suite through the 1980s and 1990s, but when it released its Office 97 version, it found that the market had become less cooperative. Many users didn't need the latest round of new features, and the upgrade cycle ground to a near halt. In the end, in fact, unhappy customers forced Microsoft to issue a special converter program enabling Office 97 files to be opened in Office 95, thus allowing them to hang on to their old software.[20] Microsoft Office had overshot a large segment of its customers.

As with hardware, the tendency to overshoot opens the door for cheap, commodity versions of applications. That explains, in large measure, the increasing popularity of open-source software. Although early versions of open-source programs tend to be clunky, lacking sophisticated user interfaces and requiring much tinkering, their customer base grows steadily as the programs' capabilities advance and become more standardized. Already, the leading Web server software is the open-source Apache, holding a 65 percent share of the market,[21] and the Linux operating system continues to steal share from Windows and proprietary Unix-based systems. In database software, the open-source MySQL is making inroads against traditional, higher-priced programs from Oracle, IBM, and Microsoft. A number of open-source applications are also being developed or refined, including free office productivity suites like OpenOffice, whose files are compatible with those of Microsoft Office. There's little reason to doubt that, as their capabilities advance, many of these applications will also begin to supplant more expensive packaged programs from traditional vendors.

Sometimes, in fact, the spread of free software is actively promoted by established companies because it's seen as a way to undermine competitors. When IBM announced in 2000 that it would support Linux, for example, one of its main motivations was to lead customers away from the operating systems of Microsoft and Sun, two of its archrivals. SAP had a similar goal in mind when, in 2003, it began distributing MySQL to its customers. The enterprise-software giant would like nothing better than to loosen the control of Oracle, IBM, and Microsoft over the databases on which SAP software runs. Sun, for its part, is heavily promoting its inexpensive StarOffice application suite, a version of the open-source OpenOffice, in hopes of eroding Microsoft's grip on the PC desktop. Information technology vendors are more than happy to see the products of their rivals turn into commodities.

Another spur to software commoditization is the increasing sophistication of the tools software writers use. To program a mainframe in the early 1950s, a software engineer had to write instructions in machine code—the actual binary numbers that computers read. By the 1960s, the development of software languages like Fortran, Cobol, and Basic allowed programmers to work at a higher level, writing in more natural formats that resembled algebraic equations or even speech. More recently, graphical software tools, like Microsoft's Virtual Basic, and object-oriented languages, like Sun's Java, have further simplified development by making it easier for programmers to reuse modules of code that perform specific tasks. Modularization makes it possible for programmers to quickly replicate—or surpass—the functionality of existing programs, further eroding the attractiveness of static, proprietary software.

By simplifying software development, the introduction of new tools has also helped to steadily expand the supply of programmers, which in the past was often a constraint on software development and replication. In 1957, there were probably fewer than twenty thousand professional software writers in the world. Today, there are an estimated nine million.[22] One of the most important trends in software development, in fact, is the rapid shift of production toward countries with low-cost labor, particularly India. General Electric already uses some eight thousand Indian contractors to write code and otherwise help operate its IT systems; approximately half of the company's software development now takes place in India.[23] GE is far from alone. Forrester Research predicts that by 2015, nearly half a million U.S. IT jobs will shift overseas as companies seek to cut their costs.[24] As the *Financial Times* puts it, "IT staff in offshore locations such as India, the Philippines, and Mexico are at least as skilled as their counterparts in the high wage economies of North America and Europe—and can cost up to 90 percent less to employ."[25]

The increasing use of lower-paid overseas workers to write code echoes, of course, the earlier shift of manufacturing capacity offshore. And the parallels go even deeper. As the software requirements of companies become more standardized and software itself becomes more modular, the development of code is coming to look less like a creative service and more like a manufacturing routine. Indeed, Kumar Mahadeva, the chief executive of Cognizant, one of the leading IT outsourcing firms, proudly calls his company's software-development operation in India "a factory," claiming that its rigid production processes and quality-control measures provide dramatically greater efficiency than traditional methods of software production.[26] Certainly there will always be a need for the creative genius in software development, but in the future it appears likely that most corporate software will be a commodity good churned out by anonymous factory workers spread across the globe.

The Internet, it's important to note, has played a critical role in accelerating the commoditization of IT. As an open network, the Internet has encouraged further standardization and in many cases increased the penalties of using proprietary, closed systems. But more than that, it has become a universal platform for making and distributing software. The Internet made it possible for programmers around the world to collaborate on open-source projects, and it opened the door to bringing overseas workers into corporate software-development efforts.

When confronted with the historical trend of increasing commoditization of software programs, including highly sophisticated business applications, some IT professionals resist the evidence. Adhering to the traditional view of software, they argue that exciting new programs will always emerge, that the malleability of software ensures unending innovation. That's not untrue, but it's almost beside the point. Yes, software innovations will continue to appear and some may be widely adopted, but that doesn't mean that individual companies will be able to hold them as proprietary resources. The trends in software design don't just ensure the commoditization of existing applications; they ensure that the functionality of any new application will be quickly copied and widely disseminated. Attractive new programs, like attractive old ones, will become costs of doing business, as the pace of commoditization continues to accelerate.

Ultimately, software, like hardware, may simply disappear. Rather than launch particular software programs, business users may simply plug into "the grid," gaining immediate access to whatever tools they need at that particular moment. Applications, in this view of the future, will be delivered over the Internet by utilities that will charge fees according to usage. Again, this may seem far-fetched. But the combination of the broadband Internet and software programs that can run on any equipment (such as those written in Java) are already making the utility model a reality in some areas. Salesforce.com, for example, provides customer relationship management applications over the Internet for a low monthly fee. Its users, who already number nearly one hundred thousand, don't need to install or maintain complex CRM packages. They just have to launch a browser and tap into Salesforce.com's servers and services. The company's slogan— "Success, Not Software"—may herald the final step in business software's brisk march toward commoditization: from in-house programs to contractor-written applications to packaged applications to fee-based services.

Innovation in the Architecture

IT does not consist only of discrete hardware and software products, of course. It also encompasses the way these components meld together to form a broader "architecture" for information management. Far from being static, the IT architecture continues to change and advance, particularly as vendors and users adapt their systems to the Internet. This fact distinguishes IT from earlier infrastructural technologies, which tended to arrive at a fairly stable architecture relatively early in their development. As the IT experts John Hagel and John Seely Brown have written, "Far from settling down into a dominant design or architecture [like earlier technologies], IT has crashed through several generations of architectures and continues to generate new ones."[27]

The question is, will technical advances in IT architecture provide defensible advantages to individual companies, or will they rapidly be incorporated into the shared infrastructure and thus be available and affordable to all? Answering that question returns us to the concept of vendorization. As closed, private networks have been eclipsed by open, public ones, it has become counterproductive for individual companies to continue to develop proprietary IT architectures. As a result, most architectural advances now emerge from vendors, who have enormous economic and competitive incentives to promote the broad adoption of their innovations, turning them into industry standards.

Consider, for example, one critical element of the IT architecture: the way people and devices connect with networks. Over the last few years, we have seen a rapid shift from wired connections, using, usually, Ethernet cables, to wireless ones, using, usually, Wi-Fi antennas. Wi-Fi, which stands for "wireless fidelity," is one of many technology advances that have earned the title Next Big Thing from the press, and in this case the moniker is well deserved. Wireless connections provide far greater flexibility to users and are often much cheaper to install and maintain than wired networks.

But far from being a potential source of advantage for an individual company, Wi-Fi is already a commodity, a cheap and increasingly universal element of the general infrastructure. How this happened—and so quickly—is illuminating because it reveals the enormous pressure to commoditize IT advances. Wi-Fi technology was developed in the mid-1990s, and by the end of the decade a relatively small company,

Intersil, was the leading producer of the semiconductors required to process Wi-Fi signals. But as soon as it became clear that Wi-Fi had broad commercial potential, Intel raced into the market and began selling its own Centrino brand of Wi-Fi chips at cut-rate prices. In 1999, according to the *Wall Street Journal,* a Wi-Fi chip cost approximately $50, but by mid-2003 Intel was selling its Centrino chip for about $20, losing, by one estimate, between $9 and $27 on each sale.

Why was Intel happy to sell Wi-Fi chips at a loss? For one thing, removing the profits from the market would destroy an upstart rival. But there was a deeper reason as well. The broad availability of Wi-Fi networks would encourage companies and individuals to buy portable laptop computers instead of stationary desktop machines, and Intel makes far more money on the chipsets for laptops than on the chipsets for desktops. It's in Intel's strategic interest, in other words, to see that Wi-Fi rapidly becomes a commodity. As an Intel executive told the *Journal,* "We're trying to remove the cost equation [from Wi-Fi adoption]."[28] At the same time, competition among telephone companies and other wireless service providers is making wireless access cheap and easy, with Wi-Fi "hot spots" proliferating in restaurants, hotels, office parks, and universities. The intense rivalry among IT vendors ensures that nearly all architectural innovations become broadly available at low prices.

A potentially more far-reaching shift in the IT architecture is toward what has come to be called "Web services." Although the term has been defined in many different ways, often depending on the commercial interests of its promoters,

Web services are essentially a set of software standards and applications that enable diverse IT systems to communicate over the Internet. In effect, Web services add a standardized interface to heterogeneous systems, allowing them to connect and share data and applications without requiring modifications to their internal workings. Closely related to grid computing, Web services promise to erase the incompatibilities among existing corporate computers and applications, allowing them to interoperate more or less seamlessly. The rise of such a "service-oriented architecture," as it's come to be called, would be a godsend for many companies, enabling them to much more easily integrate their so-called legacy systems. More broadly, though, the architecture would provide a platform for the distribution of software applications as "services" over the Internet; a company would be able to quickly reconfigure its IT systems by automatically cobbling together application modules from various outside suppliers.

That's the theory, anyway. It remains to be seen how fully the service-oriented architecture can or will actually be implemented. Enormous technical and political challenges, from establishing complex, robust data standards to ensuring security and reliability, remain to be met.[29] But the fact that some companies are already installing rudimentary forms of Web services, together with the enormous investments that vendors are devoting to the concept, indicates that at least some elements of Web-services technology will be incorporated into the general IT infrastructure.

Here, too, however, the technical innovations are coming from vendors, not users. To the extent that a service-oriented architecture is demonstrated to have value in business, both the architecture and the services distributed through it can be expected to be made rapidly available to all companies. Indeed, by shifting more control over business applications to outside service providers, Web services could come to mark the culmination of the trend toward utility-supplied IT capabilities. That's not to say that individual firms wouldn't have opportunities to *use* the new infrastructure in distinctive ways, at least in the short run.[30] But as history shows, even the uses of a new technological infrastructure become homogenized as best practices are rapidly disseminated and emulated.[31]

Whatever the particular fate of Web services, architectural innovations will continue to appear in one form or another as vendors compete to make the IT infrastructure a more stable, flexible, and reliable conduit for business. The benefits of these advances will be great, but they will tend to be broadly and quickly shared. Sun Microsystems CEO Scott McNealy uses a revealing automotive analogy to describe the evolution in corporate IT architectures. He says that in the past a company had to build its "own custom jalopy," buying various pieces of hardware and software and assembling them into a proprietary architecture for its own use. Today, however, we've progressed to the dawn of a new era, McNealy says, in which companies will simply hire "a taxi service," renting a readymade, integrated architecture from an outside vendor.[32] Such a shift promises considerable gains in performance and affordability, but it diminishes the strategic importance of the architecture. It might have cost a lot to build a custom jalopy, but at least you had a chance to build a better one than your

competitors. Hailing a taxi is something everyone can do
equally well.

When Enough's Enough

One of the founding myths of the IT business is that it will
never become a mature industry—that technological progress
has no bounds, and acts of innovation can and will demolish
all barriers to growth and success. Even as Google's Eric
Schmidt pieces together his own company's systems from
cheap components, he proclaims that the only way for IT
vendors to emerge from their early 2000s slump "is to come
up with grand new visions, which we're particularly good
at." [33] The sense of perpetual youth is an appropriate, perhaps
even necessary, myth for a business powered by restless entre-
preneurship and relentless competition. But it is just a myth.

Despite the millions of powerful microchips, the endless
miles of fiber-optic cable, and the billions of lines of intricate
code, the commercial IT infrastructure is not really all that
complicated at a conceptual level. It requires mechanisms for
storing digital data in large quantities, for quickly transporting
the data to where it's needed, and for enabling users to access
and process the data to accomplish the various practical tasks
necessary to run a business. At some point, the existing hardware and software will be sufficient—they will carry out most
of the necessary functions well enough for most purposes—
and further advances will appeal to ever narrower slices of
users, providing ever finer and more fleeting advantages.

That point may, in fact, already lie behind us. Northwest-
ern University economist Robert Gordon, in a 2000 article

published in the *Journal of Economic Perspectives,* argues that companies tend to achieve the greatest gains in the earliest stages of computer automation, after which the practical benefits of further technological advances decline abruptly. Gordon's analysis leads him to suggest that "a second distinguishing feature of the development of the computer industry, after the decline in price, is the unprecedented speed with which diminishing returns set in." It may well be, he concludes, "that the most important uses of computers were developed more than a decade into the past, not currently." [34]

That view is by no means limited to the ivory tower. Many business executives are placing a priority on making effective use of existing IT assets while shying away from aggressive spending on new technologies. Their thinking, too, reflects a growing sense that IT investments have crossed the point of diminishing returns. Tony Comper, the chairman and CEO of BMO Financial Group, one of the largest North American financial institutions, estimates that "the two main end-users in my organization—customers and employees—actually utilize about 20 percent of their computing capabilities (and I'm being generous here). The rest of the investment is mostly wasted." That leads him to "a greater truth" about IT today: "[L]ike most A-list organizations, BMO Financial Group has just about all the basic technologies we need to successfully compete right now." [35]

Such a conclusion will be anathema to those in the IT industry who have convinced themselves that IT's benefits will escalate indefinitely. [36] But it's hardly bad news. To say that IT's greatest business innovations lie in the past is not

to say that the industry has failed but rather that it has succeeded. Through entrepreneurial zeal, fearless innovation,
and an indomitable spirit of adventure, the industry has produced, in remarkably short order, a new business infrastructure that can now be used by all companies to deliver benefits
to all people. No doubt we'll continue to see useful and
sometimes amazing elaborations of the infrastructure, just as
we have with rail technology, electricity, and telephone service. And many of these advances will quickly be adopted
throughout entire industries, leading to higher productivity,
better products, and happier customers. But the innovations
won't change the essential commodity nature of information
technology. And they won't alter the new reality of IT's role
in business.

CHAPTER 4

Vanishing Advantage

Information Technology's
Changing Role in Business

IN THE MID-1990S, at the dawn of the great Internet gold rush, two academic studies appeared that examined the connection between information technology and competitive advantage. The first, published in *MIS Quarterly* in 1996, was by Erik Brynjolfsson and Lorin Hitt of the Massachusetts Institute of Technology.[1] Brynjolfsson and Hitt had earlier conducted a groundbreaking study of the impact of information technology investments on business productivity, which concluded that computer systems did, at least eventually, lead to gains in productivity.[2] They then decided to see what happened to those productivity gains: Were companies able to hold onto them, in the form of higher profits, or were they competed away, ending up in the pockets of customers?

The two researchers sifted through data on IT spending and financial performance from 370 large U.S. companies. They first looked at whether the spending had changed the companies' productivity, and, confirming their earlier conclusions, they found considerable evidence that it indeed had. They discovered, they wrote, "strong support for the hypothesis that IT has contributed positively to total output." Even when they took into account the cost of capital, they found that IT investments usually produced "high rates of return" through improved productivity.[3]

But when they looked at how the economic benefits of the enhanced productivity were actually distributed, they found strong indications that it was consumers who ended up with the lion's share. Their examination of company financial data "showed little evidence of an impact of IT on supranormal profitability" and indeed suggested "the possibility of an overall negative effect of IT on profitability."[4] Consumers, however, appeared to receive substantial economic benefits from companies' investments in IT. In conclusion, the researchers reported that "our profitability results suggest that, on average, firms are making the IT investments necessary to maintain competitive parity but are not able to gain competitive advantage."[5]

The second study appeared the next year. Undertaken by Baba Prasad and Patrick Harker at the Wharton School at the University of Pennsylvania, it examined the impact of IT capital spending on business performance in the U.S. banking industry. Because of the enormous quantity of transactions banks have to process, they have invested particularly heavily in IT, and the complexity of their businesses has led many of them to develop highly customized applications. If IT were going to have a strong influence on competitive advantage, one would think it should be apparent in banking. Yet in combing through detailed data on 47 major U.S. retail banks, Prasad and Harker found no evidence that spending on IT capital had enhanced profitability, as measured by either return on assets or return on equity. Indeed, they found that the spending had not even boosted productivity, as the costs of installing the systems outweighed the resulting gains in performance. Information technology, although a competitive necessity, brings banks no strategic benefit, they concluded. "The easy availability of IT to all banks implies that IT investments do not provide any competitive advantage," the researchers wrote at the end of their report. "IT investment has zero or insignificant effect on bank profitability."[6]

Outside of scholarly circles, the two studies went largely unnoticed. At the time, business gurus, management consultants, and technology reporters were all happily pronouncing the death of the "Old Economy" and proclaiming the coming hegemony of the digital business model. It seemed obvious that the future of commerce would be written in software code. Today, however, the researchers' findings seem to have greater resonance than all the overheated rhetoric of the late 1990s. Although the studies looked at average results rather than the experiences of particular firms, they were among the first clear signs that companies tend not to be successful in defending competitive advantages gained through IT innovations. The research indicated that IT's strategic potential might be quite limited and that, like earlier infrastructural technologies, IT might rapidly turn into a simple cost of doing business.[7]

Given the characteristics of both hardware and software that push them toward rapid standardization and commoditization, such findings should not come as a surprise. Indeed, the evolution of IT's role in business has closely mirrored the pattern established by earlier infrastructural technologies. The buildout of the IT infrastructure, for example, has been every bit as breathtaking as that of the railroads or the telegraph system. Consider just a few statistics. During the last quarter of the twentieth century, the computational power of a microprocessor increased by a factor of 66,000.[8] Spending on software jumped from less than $1 billion in 1970 to $138 billion in 2000.[9] In the dozen years between 1989 and 2001, the number of host computers connected to the Internet grew from 80,000 to more than 125 million. Over the last ten years, the number of sites on the World Wide Web has grown from zero to nearly 40 million.[10] And since the 1980s, more than 280 million miles of fiber-optic cable have been laid, enough, as *Business Week* has noted, to "circle the earth 11,320 times." [11] Sustained, intense investment has brought sophisticated information technology within the reach of every sizeable company in the developed world.

That doesn't mean that all businesses have embraced the new technologies at the same rate. The process by which an infrastructural technology becomes a shared and standardized resource is an organic and evolutionary one. It proceeds at a different pace in different industries and different countries, depending on operational and competitive characteristics, available capital, government regulations, and many other factors. In the United States, for example, the financial services industry has been an early and heavy investor in IT, with well-capitalized banks, insurance companies, and brokerage houses moving quickly to automate their transaction-intensive businesses. But the fragmented health care industry, shielded from competition, has been relatively slow to adopt IT, despite its complex information- and transaction-processing requirements. Today, therefore, IT continues to hold considerably more potential for providing competitive advantage for health care providers than it does for financial institutions. But even allowing for these natural variations, history shows that in general IT's strategic role has diminished rapidly and inexorably.

When IT Was New

As with earlier infrastructural technologies, IT provided quick-moving and forward-looking companies with many opportunities for sustainable competitive advantage early in its buildout, when it could still be "owned" like a proprietary technology. Sometimes the advantages were based on superior access to new hardware and software, sometimes on superior insight into IT's use or transformational power, and sometimes on a combination of better access and greater foresight.

The earliest access barrier was technical. Since no business computers existed before the 1950s, a company that wanted one had to, literally, build its own. That's what the British tea-shop operator J. Lyons & Company did. In 1947, the company's directors, long known for their innovative business practices, realized they could gain an edge on competitors by automating routine office functions like payroll management as well as more complex operational processes like inventory management. The company organized two teams of technically adept employees, one to build the computer, the other to write the software. Four years later, the company's groundbreaking computer—dubbed LEO, for Lyons Electronic Office—became operational. Installed in Lyons's London headquarters—in "a room the size of a tennis court," according to one report[12]—the enormous machine, outfitted with five thousand vacuum tubes to carry out calculations and several long, mercury-filled cylinders to store data, gave Lyons an information-processing advantage that its rivals couldn't match for years. Not only was the company able to reduce the time required to process an employee's weekly pay from eight minutes to less than two seconds, it was also able to more efficiently order supplies and distribute goods; and, for the first time, it could track the costs and profits of individual products and shops on a daily basis.

Few other companies had the skill, or the nerve, to build their own computers. But such heroic efforts soon became unnecessary, anyway. While Lyons was toiling away on its own mainframe, big electronics and business-machine companies were slowly coming to appreciate the commercial potential of computers. In 1951, the same year the LEO went into operation, Remington Rand introduced its UNIVAC, the first electronic, programmable computer to be offered to the general business market. Within a few years, other large suppliers—National Cash Register, General Electric, Philco, RCA, Burroughs, and, most important, IBM—had also begun building mainframes for businesses.

As computers became readily available, the technical barrier to commercial computing began to disappear. But there remained a daunting economic barrier. Only large and wealthy companies could afford to buy or lease a mainframe computer and maintain the technical staff capable of operating it. The early UNIVACs, for instance, cost upward of $1 million apiece. And when IBM introduced its first line of business computers— the 700 series—in 1952, each one cost more than $150,000 a year to rent.[13] At the time, only a few dozen businesses could afford outlays of that magnitude.

But however expensive the hardware, it was software development that presented the highest access barriers. Because computer manufacturers paid little attention to software, companies had to assemble their own programming staffs, a very expensive proposition. And even if a company had the money to hire the necessary programmers, it often had difficulty recruiting them. People skilled in the arcane art of writing machine code were at the time few and far between, and they tended to work for the military.

Of course, the very difficulty of creating information systems meant that any company able to pull off the feat could open a wide gulf between itself and its rivals. A breakthrough in corporate data processing could take many years for competitors to replicate. Perhaps the most famous example of a company gaining such an early-mover advantage is American Airlines with its Sabre reservation system. American began discussing the possibility of building a computerized reservation system with IBM in 1953. At the time, reservations for airplane flights were made through a cumbersome, largely manual process that was both labor-intensive and error-prone. Information on seat assignments was kept separately from details about passengers, requiring a complicated round of reconcilement that added more costs and more mistakes. To handle all the data, each major airline had to maintain a vast reservations office that, according to one account, resembled "a war operations room." [14] Although American had installed a rudimentary mechanical system for tracking seat assignments, called the Reservisor, it still depended largely on the traditional, cumbersome manual process.

The airline saw that improving the reservations process could provide enormous competitive benefits. First, an automated system would dramatically reduce labor costs. Second, a reduction in errors would allow the airline to reduce its "safety stock" of empty seats on each flight, significantly boosting revenues. Third, as reservations became more reliable and easier to make, customers would come to prefer flying on American rather than other airlines. And finally, a centralized, computerized system would enable American to analyze its operations with much greater precision, leading to smarter decisions about routes, planes, services, and fares.

In the mid-1950s, however, computer hardware and software had not advanced to the point where such a complex, real-time system was possible. But it was becoming increasingly clear that the necessary technology would soon be available. In 1959, after six years of exploratory analysis, American's president, C. R. Smith, took the leap and signed a contract for developing the necessary software, to be run on dual IBM 7090 mainframes. It was a massive and risky undertaking, requiring 200 skilled engineers and technicians five years to complete and costing American an estimated $30 million, a staggering sum at the time.

But when the first test installations of the system began to be rolled out in 1962, it immediately became clear that Sabre would fulfill its potential and become a competitive boon for the airline. The productivity gain was striking: Sabre could process in a few minutes the number of transactions that used to take dozens of clerks a full day to get through. At the same time, the error rate dropped from 8 percent to less than 1 percent.[15] And, as expected, the data produced by the system gave American new flexibility in allocating its resources and new precision in setting its prices. It's been estimated that the financial gains from the system enabled the airline to earn a 25 percent return on its huge investment.[16] But the marketing benefits were equally great. As the *Wall Street Journal's* Thomas Petzinger reports in his book *Hard Landing,* "Almost immediately American began gaining market share on the other airlines, including its archrival, United Airlines." In the wake of American's achievement, Petzinger continues, any airline that "ignored the computer revolution did so at tremendous peril."[17]

Of course, few airlines did ignore the computer revolution. Most of American's competitors quickly saw the advantage

American had gained and immediately launched their own efforts to install reservation systems. IBM, for its part, was all too happy to help. Drawing on its experience with Sabre, the computer giant created a generic system, called PARS, that it peddled to other airlines with considerable success. By the early 1970s, a number of PARS-based systems, most notably United's Apollo, were widely seen as technically superior to Sabre. But American's head start proved too great to overcome. By the end of the 1970s, American had succeeded in making Sabre the dominant reservation system used by travel agents, providing the airline with an important new source of revenue as well as an often decisive marketing advantage on hotly contested routes.

Locking in Advantage

Sabre is an example of an advantage derived mainly from superior access to an infrastructural technology early in its development. Other airlines appreciated the potential value of automating reservations—the problems with the existing manual process were painfully obvious—but it was American that made the investments necessary to surmount the technical and cost barriers.

In addition to the access advantages, there were also many foresight advantages to be gained from IT during its build-out. A classic example of a company having a superior understanding of how IT could serve as the basis for new operating processes was American Hospital Supply. Founded in Chicago in 1922, AHS grew steadily over the years to become one of the leading makers and distributors of medical supplies in the United States. In the early 1960s, it also became a pioneer in information systems.[18] At the time, AHS, like other sellers of medical goods, would take orders by sending a crew of salesmen out to hospitals. At the end of each day, the salesmen would write out their order forms and mail them back to company headquarters, where they'd be reviewed, sorted, and forwarded to the appropriate manufacturing or distribution facilities. The manual ordering process was slow and expensive, as the average hospital placed some 50,000 orders a year, often through as many as ten different buyers. As computers began to be more common in business, AHP realized that it might be possible to connect the hospital buyers directly to its distribution operations through electronic linkages, bypassing the traditional order-taking process altogether. Such a system would not only dramatically reduce AHS's costs; it would enable the company to deliver far better service to its customers.

To test the concept, AHS quickly cobbled together a primitive network, installing an IBM Dataphone in the purchasing department of one large West Coast hospital and connecting a card-punch machine to a telephone line in one of its distribution centers. When the buyers at the hospital fed a coded punch card into the Dataphone, a copy was automatically produced at the distribution center, where it was fed into an IBM billing machine that produced a packing list and an invoice. The system was a success, enabling orders to be filled much more quickly and accurately. Soon, 200 more hospitals asked for similar systems.

By the mid-1970s, the rudimentary system had evolved into a much more sophisticated one, which AHS called Analytic Systems Automated Purchasing, or ASAP. Developed in-house, ASAP used proprietary software running on a mainframe computer, and hospital purchasing agents communicated with it through terminals and printers at their sites. Because more efficient ordering enabled hospitals to reduce their inventories—and thus their costs—customers were quick to embrace the system. And because it was proprietary to AHS, it effectively locked out competitors. For several years, in fact, AHS was the only distributor offering electronic ordering, an advantage that led to years of market gains and superior financial results. From 1978 to 1983, as the company rolled out new versions of ASAP that provided ever tighter links with customers' inventory control systems, AHS's sales and profits rose robustly, at annual rates of 13 percent and 18 percent, respectively.[19]

AHS, like American Airlines before it, gained a true competitive advantage by capitalizing on characteristics of infrastructural technologies that are common in the early stages of their buildout, in particular their high cost, technical complexity, and lack of standardization. Within a decade, however, those barriers to competition were crumbling. The arrival of personal computers and packaged software, together with the emergence of networking standards, was rendering proprietary communication systems unattractive to their users and uneconomic to their owners. Indeed, in an ironic, if predictable, twist, the closed nature and outdated technology of AHS's system turned it from a source of advantage to a source of disadvantage. By the dawn of the 1990s, after AHS had merged with Baxter Travenol to form Baxter International, the company's senior executives had come to view ASAP as, according to a Harvard Business School case study, "a millstone around their necks."[20] Nevertheless, AHS's system provided a competitive edge that lasted more than a decade, no doubt paying for itself several times over. The company's decision to pioneer electronic ordering systems was a brilliant business move, even if the edge it provided did not last forever.

In addition to transforming particular business processes, like ordering and fulfillment, IT would also transform entire industries and bring new ones into existence. Here, again, superior foresight could lead to tremendous competitive advantages, as the history of Reuters shows. Reuters had been a pioneer of communication technology since its founding in the mid-1800s. Its first breakthrough, in 1849, was decidedly low-tech: It used pigeons to carry stock quotes across the gap between the end of the Belgian telegraph line in Brussels and the start of the German line in Aachen. Two years later, it became a telegraph agency, sending price information over the new English Channel cable connecting London and Paris. In the early twentieth century, it was one of the first companies to use radio and teleprinters to transmit news, and in 1964 it began to use computers to speed the communication of financial information.

Perhaps its greatest technological triumph came in the early 1970s. At the time, countries were beginning to abandon the fixed-rate currency system that had been in place since the Bretton Woods conference of 1944. Reuters saw

that once rates began to fluctuate freely, a vibrant foreign exchange market would emerge, and it would require extremely
rapid communication of information on prices and trading.
The telephones and telexes traditionally used by traders
wouldn't be able to process the vast amount of information at
the necessary speed.

Reuters stepped into the competitive breach with its
groundbreaking Reuter Monitor Money Rates service. The
company installed dedicated terminals in banks, corporate offices, and other trading houses, in effect creating an electronic
marketplace under its control. The proprietary network became the dominant trading mechanism for currency, providing Reuters with a vast new source of revenues and profits. It
also served as a launching pad for many new information
services, from bond quotes to news headlines, providing
Reuters with a platform for rapid revenue and profit growth
for two decades. During the 1980s, Reuters' pre-tax profits
shot up from £3.9 million to £283.1 million.[21]

The Technology Replication Cycle

Some commentators have argued that IT itself has never
been the basis for competitive advantage—that advantage
comes not from the technology but only from "how you use
it." But while such a claim could accurately be made about
any business asset—if a company does not know how to use
the asset well, it is unlikely to gain an edge—it is nevertheless
misleading. As the stories of J. Lyons, American Airlines,
American Hospital Supply, and Reuters reveal, distinctive information systems could and did provide the foundation for

very strong and durable advantages during the buildout of the IT infrastructure. The systems themselves formed daunting barriers to competitors. Yet the stories also reveal why IT-based advantages have become harder and harder to achieve and sustain as the infrastructure has matured.

Being a first mover in information technology is expensive. American Airlines had to make a massive investment, in both money and time, to create Sabre. The airlines that followed in its wake could spend less to get more. For one thing, the followers were able to learn from American's experience, avoiding many of the costly trials and errors that the pioneer had to slog through. Also, instead of building their systems entirely from scratch, as American had to, the followers were able to draw on standardized technologies developed and sold by the vendor—IBM—that had helped American build its system. Finally, the extraordinarily rapid pace of IT advances ensured that latecomers would also be able to match or exceed the first mover's performance at a far lower price.

It was only because it took the followers a considerable amount of time to launch their own systems that American's early investment paid off. If competitors had been able to replicate Sabre's capabilities sooner, at a lower cost, they would have quickly undermined American's lead, and American almost certainly would have failed to recoup its huge investment. As the Sabre case shows, it's not enough simply to gain a technological advantage. All distinctive uses of technology are eventually copied. The real challenge is to be able to sustain the advantage long enough to earn a solid return on your investment or, if possible, to leverage the technological advantage into more durable advantages—superior scale, say, or a better-known brand.

If a company is unable to hold onto a technological advantage for a substantial period, its early-mover strategy can backfire. Competitors won't just catch up; they'll leapfrog the first mover, introducing more powerful systems. As American Hospital Supply eventually discovered, an information system can be very difficult to replace once it's been embedded in a business. A first mover whose system is quickly surpassed by competitors' systems may, as a result, find that its outsized investment has not only failed to provide an advantage but has left it burdened with an outdated technology—a millstone—that places it at an ever growing disadvantage.

The time it takes for competitors to copy a new technology—what might be called the *technology replication cycle*—is the crucial variable in gauging the strategic power of an IT investment. And the history of IT reveals one overarching truth: The technology replication cycle gets shorter and shorter. As the performance of hardware and software improves, as their cost falls, and as knowledge about them spreads, competitors become able to match the capabilities and performance of new systems at an ever faster clip. That means, in turn, that the likelihood of an early investment in a new technology truly paying off—something of a long shot to begin with, given the risk involved—gets ever slimmer as time goes by. Today, most IT-based competitive advantages simply vanish too quickly to be meaningful.

Rapid price deflation is a salient characteristic of all infrastructural technologies, but with computing it has been particularly dramatic. When Gordon Moore made his famously prescient assertion that the density of circuits on a computer chip would double about every two years, he was making a prediction about the coming explosion in processing power. But he was also making a prediction about the coming free-fall in the price of computer functionality. The cost of computing power has dropped relentlessly, from $480 per million instructions per second (MIPS) in 1978 to $50 per MIPS in 1985 to $4 per MIPS in 1995—a trend that continues unabated.[22] A megabyte of disk storage cost $10,000 dollars in 1956; with that money today, you can buy 20 Dell desktop computers, each with a 40-gigabyte hard drive.[23] Similar declines have occurred in the cost of data transmission. Overall, according to a study by researchers at MIT and Wharton, the cost of corporate data processing has dropped by more than 99.9 percent since the 1960s.[24] The rapidly increasing affordability of IT functionality has not only democratized the computer revolution, it has destroyed one of the most important potential barriers to replication. Even the most cutting-edge IT capabilities rapidly become available to all.

Another once-strong barrier to replication was the proprietary network. If a company was able to be the first to establish proprietary links to customers or suppliers, those links became extremely difficult for rivals to break. It was usually very costly for partners to abandon an existing network and install and learn to use another one. American, AHS, and Reuters all benefited by locking in, respectively, travel agents, hospital buyers, and currency traders to private networks. The rise of open networks, particularly the Internet, has, however, undermined the efficacy of proprietary networks. An open network's low cost and high flexibility make it an attractive substitute for almost all rigid connections, and most companies have acted quickly to move their on-line transactions onto the Internet. Where proprietary connections remain, such as in longstanding electronic data interchange (EDI) networks, it's rarely because they offer any company an advantage anymore. It's simply because the costs and risks of shifting to the Internet have not yet dropped far enough to justify breaking the lock.[25]

Networking promotes replication in another important way as well. Because IT capabilities tend to be more valuable when shared than when used in isolation, competitors will sometimes work together to develop and promote the use of an attractive new system. They'll replicate the technology on purpose, sacrificing the possibility of competitive differentiation in order to increase overall productivity. That was what happened with barcoding. Grocery retailers, realizing that a universal barcode-scanning system could dramatically reduce their costs, created an industry consortium in the early 1970s to choose a common coding format and establish technical standards. When the consortium picked the IBM-developed Universal Product Code as the standard, big grocery chains quickly abandoned the various custom checkout methods they had developed and embraced the UPC.

The rollout of a more recent IT innovation—Internet banking—provides a particularly striking example of how the acceleration of the technology replication cycle works against pioneers. In 1995 and 1996, several banks rushed to create proprietary on-line banking systems for customers, hoping that the new channel would distinguish them from competitors (while also fending off Internet start-ups). As it turned out, however, consumers were slow to embrace on-line banking—it proved less enticing to them than the banks had expected. By the time a critical mass of customers began using the new channel, Internet banking had already become a commonplace, and usually free, service offered by most banks. And because the cost of introducing on-line banking had fallen quickly and sharply as vendors moved in to offer generic packaged systems, the late movers were able to match the pioneers' capabilities at a far lower cost. The pioneers had not only failed to gain an advantage; they had wasted a lot of money.

The Homogenization of Processes

In yet another echo of earlier infrastructural technologies, the buildout of the IT infrastructure has not just standardized the technology but also many aspects of its use. A hundred years ago, vendors of machine tools incorporated sophisticated manufacturing processes into the design of their tools, enabling those processes to be shared by all companies. In the same way, software makers today constantly build the most advanced business practices into their programs. Indeed, it could be argued that as business systems become more sophisticated, vendors compete less on the technology of their offerings than on their ability to stay on the cutting edge of industry best practices.

This is particularly true of enterprise systems. Unlike earlier software packages that tended to automate a specific activity such as typing or billing, enterprise software automates an entire process—often one of the core processes of a business. At the same time, the software imposes constraints on the process; it influences, or even determines, how the process proceeds. When a company buys, for instance, a Seibel software package for customer relationship management, it is also buying the Seibel way of managing customers. The software and the practice become indistinguishable.

IT scholar Thomas Davenport explained this phenomenon well in a 1998 *Harvard Business Review* article on ERP systems: "When developing information systems in the past, companies would first decide how they wanted to do business and then choose a software package that would support their proprietary processes. They often rewrote large portions of the software code to ensure a tight fit. With enterprise systems, however, the sequence is reversed. The business often must be modified to fit the system."[26] The good news is that the generic process often reflects the state of the art in process design—replicating the best processes is crucial to a vendor's success. The bad news is that it's a generic process; because it standardizes the use of a technology, it provides little room for a company to distinguish itself. It's revealing, if not surprising, that in the late 1990s enterprise systems came to be called "companies in a box."[27]

Why do companies make such a trade-off? Once again, it's usually for the same reason they buy any goods or services from outside vendors: Because the cost savings of a standardized, purchased resource come to outweigh the differentiation advantages of a custom resource created in-house. A writer for *Inbound Logistics* displayed that logic in describing why more and more companies are buying generic logistics software: "While most companies once thought that their business processes were too unique to use configurable software (as opposed to customized software), transportation managers are quickly realizing that leveraging industry best practices far outweighs the benefit of perpetuating a unique process." [28] This is, of course, a gross overstatement; smart companies know that distinctive processes lie at the heart of competitive advantage. But when it comes to complex software applications, the economics of purchasing an off-the-shelf version have become so compelling that few companies can justify the cost and risk of building a new system from scratch.

Further accelerating the homogenization of computer systems and their use is the vast infrastructure for sharing experiences, ideas, and best practices that has grown up around the IT business. Through innumerable magazines, articles, conferences, consulting projects, and academic studies, IT knowledge is rapidly collected, codified, and disseminated throughout the business community. As IT researchers Erik Brynjolfsson and Lorin Hitt have explained, innovations in computerization "are generally not subject to any form of intellectual property protection and are widely and consciously copied, often with the aid of consulting firms, benchmarking services and business school professors. . . . Job mobility also disseminates computer-related benefits as IT professionals move from firm to firm. . . . As a result, the gains to the economy might plausibly be much larger than the private gains to the original innovator." [29]

The trend toward outsourcing key IT systems, and even the processes that run on them, will further accelerate the homogenization trend. As companies look to business process outsourcing (BPO) vendors to carry out many IT-intensive processes, from budgeting to logistics to training to customer service, they will neutralize those processes as potential sources of advantage. The processes themselves will begin to become part of the shared infrastructure.

The Emergence of Dominant Designs

Still, though, there's one more potential source of IT-based advantage: having superior insight into how IT might transform or give rise to entire industries. Here again there is a somewhat romantic view that many in the IT industry subscribe to. It goes something like this: "We are only at the beginning of the Digital Age. As great technological leaps continue to be made—in wireless networking, molecular processors, ecological computing, and so on—people will change the way they live, shop, and interact, and great waves of transformation will wash over the business world, creating vast new industries and changing old ones into unrecognizable forms—in ways no one can even predict yet."

That may be so; the future is notoriously hard to predict. But a strong argument could also be made that computing's power to create genuine industrial transformations is largely spent. Yes, we'll continue to see the occasional eBay—we always have—and some industries, like the music business, remain in real flux as a result of the ubiquity of information technology. But history shows that the transformational power of an infrastructural technology dissipates as its build-out nears completion. A technology may precipitate a period of upheaval when it first emerges, but free markets are quite good at motivating entrepreneurs, managers, and investors to see and very quickly exploit the big new business opportunities. It doesn't take long for what business scholars call the "dominant design"—the optimal way of doing business that incorporates the new technology—to emerge in an industry and for all companies to adopt it.

While it's hard to say precisely when the buildout of an infrastructural technology has concluded, there are, as we've seen, many signs that the IT buildout is much closer to its end than its beginning. First, the power of IT is outstripping most of the business needs it fulfills. Second, and related, the price of essential IT functionality has dropped to the point where it is more or less affordable to all. Third, the capacity of the universal distribution network (the Internet) has caught up with demand—indeed, we already have considerably more fiber-optic capacity than we need. Fourth, leading IT vendors, from Microsoft to IBM to Hewlett-Packard to Sun, are rushing to position themselves as suppliers of "on demand" infrastructural services—as utilities, in other words.

Finally, and perhaps most tellingly, an enormous investment bubble has expanded and burst, which historically has been an indication that an infrastructural technology is reaching the end of its buildout. In her seminal book *Technological Revolutions and Financial Capital,* Carlota Perez divides the period of adoption of a new and broadly used technology into two phases. First comes the "installation period," when the

technology "advance[s] like a bulldozer disrupting the established fabric and articulating new industrial networks, setting
up new infrastructures and spreading new and superior ways
of doing things." Then comes the "deployment period,"
when the focus of innovation and adaptation shifts from the
technology itself to the surrounding institutional framework,
and capital markets and regulatory regimes are reshaped to fit
the new infrastructure. Between these two phases comes a
"turning point," which usually takes the form of an economic
recession following a period of "frantic investment in the new
industries and the infrastructure, stimulated by a stock market
boom that usually becomes a bubble."[30] The collapse of the
bubble signals that "a new infrastructure is in place" and that
"the new way of doing things with the new technologies has
become 'common sense.'"[31] At this point, the competitive
chaos settles down, and the stage is set for all companies to
share the benefits of the new infrastructure.[32]

The crash of the NASDAQ and the ensuing recession mark
such a turning point in the computerization of business.
Adapting to the new IT infrastructure will pose many challenges to private companies and public institutions for many
years to come, but the influence of the underlying technologies on competition will continue to fade. Success in the future will be less a matter of using information technology cre-
atively than of simply using it well.

5

The Universal Strategy Solvent

The IT Infrastructure's Corrosive Effect on Traditional Advantages

ALTHOUGH INFRASTRUCTURAL technologies lose much of their power to provide competitive advantage as they mature, they don't lose their power to destroy it. The rail system, for example, neutralized many of the traditional locational advantages held by companies situated near ports, mineheads, and population centers. The telegraph reduced the value of long-cultivated international business relationships built on written correspondence and confidential couriers. The establishment of the electric grid rendered obsolete old ways of manufacturing and the advantages that went with them—having the best-designed shaft-and-pulley system for distributing steam power suddenly meant nothing. The rise of the machine-tool industry blurred distinctions between the skills of individual craftsmen, endowing all factory workers with similar capabilities.

The *Mechanics Weekly* writer grasped this phenomenon intuitively as he watched the steam locomotives speed down the tracks at Rainhill in 1829. "Peculiar local advantages will figure less than they have done in our manufacturing and commercial history," he foresaw, "since whatever one place produces, can [be] as quickly and cheaply transported to another." A century and a half later, strategy scholar Michael Porter acknowledged it as a general business truth, writing in his seminal 1985 book *Competitive Advantage* that "technological change is . . . a great equalizer, eroding the competitive advantage of even well-entrenched firms and propelling others to the forefront."[1]

This neutralizing effect promises to be particularly strong with information technology. Because IT is so flexible in its application and so deeply entwined with business processes—particularly the informational processes that have supplanted physical processes at the core of modern economies—it can corrode advantages not just in one or a few areas, but across many aspects of a company's business. Any traditional advantage in prosecuting a particular activity or process, from setting type to designing componentry to providing customer service, will tend to dissipate as that activity or process is automated. As businesses adopt similar systems, best practices turn into universal practices, and performance converges.

In the late 1990s, a doctoral student at the Harvard Business School, Mark Cotteleer, documented this phenomenon in microcosm in a study of a large manufacturer's adoption of an enterprise resource planning system.[2] The company deployed a single ERP package throughout its worldwide operations, replacing a number of different systems that had been used by units in North America, Europe, and Asia. Cotteleer examined variations in the units' performance on one crucial operating measure—the speed with which they fulfilled customer orders—both before and after the installation of the system. He analyzed more than one hundred thousand order records spanning a three-year period, from twelve months before the ERP came on-line to twenty-four months after.

Before the new system was put in place, variations in order lead times among the three regions were pronounced, with Europe and Asia holding a large advantage over North America. Four months prior to the system's rollout, for example, it typically took North America 51 days to fill an order, while Europe took just 35 days and Asia just 36. The installation of a common ERP system immediately erased these differences, bringing the three regions into competitive parity. One month after the installation, the average lead times for North America, Europe, and Asia were, respectively, 29, 27, and 28 days. A year after the installation, the lead times were still tightly bunched, at 35, 33, and 37 days. Although variations in performance increased during the second year, as managerial and other local differences began to influence the units' operations, the lead times remained more homogenized than they had been before the system was adopted. Most striking, however, was the fact that two years after the system went into effect North America had become the lead-time leader. The advantage originally held by Europe and Asia had been obliterated, apparently forever.

It's not hard to see how a similar convergence of performance and corrosion of advantage would take place among different companies that adopt the same or similar information systems, particularly systems aimed at automating transaction-intensive activities. Software that automates the customer service function, distributing inquiries and information to telephone representatives, will tend, for example, to erase differences in response times and other aspects of performance as it becomes broadly adopted throughout an industry. The homogenizing effect of the IT infrastructure will intensify as companies continue to look to outside contractors to operate key systems or even entire processes—for example, when competitors close down their own call centers and transfer the function to a handful of outsourcers in, say, India.

By providing companies with a shared communication and distribution platform, the Internet has greatly magnified the homogenizing effect of IT. Not only has the Internet undercut the advantages inherent in proprietary, closed networks, but it has shifted power away from companies and toward customers, further leveling the competitive playing field. In the 1996 edition of his book *The Road Ahead,* Bill Gates hailed the Internet as a foundation for "friction-free capitalism," a new commercial infrastructure that would push markets ever closer to Adam Smith's ideal of perfect competition. The Internet, he wrote, would become the "ultimate go-between, the universal middleman," enabling customers to easily compare the prices, features, and quality of alternative products and thus spurring more intense competition among would-be suppliers. The result would be a consumer utopia: "All the goods in the world will be available for you to examine, compare, and often, customize. . . . It will be a shopper's heaven."[3] What Gates failed to point out is that a shopper's heaven is a business executive's hell. When it comes to markets, friction is often just another word for profit.

Michael Porter presented the dark side of friction-free capitalism in his controversial 2001 article "Strategy and the Internet." Surveying the business changes wrought by the Internet and their impact on competitive advantage and profitability, he concluded that

most of the trends are negative. Internet technology provides buyers with easier access to information about products and suppliers, thus bolstering buyer bargaining power. The Internet mitigates the need for such things as an established sales force or access to existing channels, reducing barriers to entry. By enabling new approaches to meeting needs and performing functions, it creates new substitutes [for existing products and processes]. Because it is an open system, companies have more difficulty maintaining proprietary offerings, thus intensifying the rivalry among competitors. The use of the Internet also tends to expand the geographic market, bringing many more companies into competition with one another. . . . The great paradox of the Internet is that its very benefits—making information widely available; reducing the difficulty of purchasing, marketing, and distribution; allowing buyers and sellers to find and transact business with one another more easily—also make it more difficult for companies to capture those benefits as profits.[4]

By erasing many traditional operating advantages and making companies' processes and prices more transparent to customers, IT threatens to become a kind of universal solvent of business strategy, speeding up the natural forces that over time push companies toward competitive parity. In assessing the implications of the IT infrastructure, therefore, executives need to look well beyond the relatively narrow confines of IT management—to the very heart of how they think about business strategy.

Sustainable Advantage and Leverageable Advantage

Some businesspeople, looking at the changeability of current business conditions and the speed of competitive replication, have jumped to the conclusion that the entire idea of strategy is becoming obsolete, that because long-term advantages are more difficult to achieve, companies shouldn't bother pursuing them at all. As the CIO of a major British financial institution recently, and amusingly, put it, "strategy is not a very strategic term right now."[5] Business success, in this view, hinges entirely on a company's flexibility and agility—on its ability to outrun and outmaneuver competitors. Managers don't need to think ahead; they just need to act. But such a belief is self-fulfilling and, in the end, self-defeating. The fact that competitive advantage has become more difficult to sustain doesn't make it less important; it makes it more important.

As buyers become more powerful and business processes and systems more homogeneous, only the strategically astute companies will be able to rise above the competitive free-for-all.

The two current paragons of long-term business success— Dell and Wal-Mart—underscore the importance of intelligent strategy. Both have been adept users of IT, and that has led some observers to conclude that technology is the source of their competitive advantage. But a closer look reveals that neither has built its advantage on technology itself. Instead, through extraordinarily disciplined approaches to business planning, each has carefully positioned itself to capture the lion's share of the profits in its industry.

Wal-Mart's strategic advantage dates from its founding in the early 1960s, when Sam Walton took a distinctive approach to both store location and merchandising. While other discount retailers were putting their stores in cities, Walton built his in rural areas. Because the locations he chose could not support more than one big store, he effectively locked out competitors, keeping the markets to himself. And instead of selling cheap nonbranded goods, like other discounters, he stocked his shelves with name-brand merchandise that he sold at cut-rate prices, a combination that drew shoppers away from traditional Main Street merchants and made trips to big-city department stores unnecessary.

To sustain its distinctive strategy, Wal-Mart has been relentless in pursuing efficiency everywhere in its operations. The company's stinginess is legendary, as is its ruthlessness in bargaining with suppliers. But it has not been shy about spending money on information systems that support its low-price strategy. In the 1980s, when the IT buildout was still fairly early in its progress, Wal-Mart assembled logistics systems that allowed it to more efficiently restock store shelves and to radically reduce the inventory it had to hold. It was also a leader in creating electronic links with large suppliers, enabling its vendors to pack and ship deliveries for individual stores. Other retailers were often able to mimic Wal-Mart's systems—the underlying technology, as MIT economist Robert Solow has pointed out, was "not especially at the technological frontiers"[6]—but because Wal-Mart's advantage lay in a complex, tightly integrated, and difficult-to-copy combination of processes and activities, competitors' IT investments went largely for naught. Wal-Mart continued to grow rapidly, to the point where its greatest edge has now become its superior scale—one of the most traditional and yet still most powerful of all competitive advantages.

Dell, too, established its strategy well before it built most of its much-praised IT systems. Its advantage lies in the distinctive direct-to-the-customer approach to selling computers it pioneered in the early 1980s. By cutting out the wholesalers and retailers that dominated computer sales at the time, Dell changed the economics of the industry. Instead of having to fill many distribution channels with expensive and rapidly depreciating finished goods, the company could wait to receive a buyer's order before actually assembling the desired computer. Because the build-to-order approach dramatically reduced the need for inventory and working capital, it was far more efficient than other makers' build-to-stock methods, allowing Dell to quickly become the low-cost provider, an enviable position in a rapidly commoditizing market. Dell's essential competitive advantage was already in place back when it was still taking customer orders over the telephone, long before it launched its now widely emulated Web store.

Much like Wal-Mart, Dell's distinctive strategy translated into rapid growth, providing the company with the scale economies necessary to maintain and strengthen its position as the low-cost producer. Dell's IT investments have actually been relatively conservative, and all have been aimed at reinforcing the efficiency of its operations, particularly its connections with suppliers and customers. It's true that IT has buttressed Dell's advantage, but it is by no means the source of that advantage. As Joan Magretta puts it in her book *What Management Is,* "Michael Dell's really powerful insights haven't been technological ones. They've been business insights."[7] That's why other computer manufacturers have been able to match Dell's systems but not its results.

The enduring success of Wal-Mart and Dell gives the lie to the idea that strategy is dead or dying. Yes, these two companies are adept at execution and savvy at using IT, but their ability to consistently outpace competitors in growth and profitability can be traced to the stability of their strategies, not to their tactical agility. It is their single-mindedness in establishing and defending their privileged industry positions that sets them apart. Indeed, Dell's one major miscue was its brief attempt to sell its machines through retailers, a shift in strategy that backfired and was soon abandoned. Far from rushing willy-nilly from one business model to another, Wal-Mart and Dell display an old-fashioned strategic steadfastness, a determination to resist change for change's sake. They don't move slowly, but they do move deliberately.

These two companies are exemplars, but they're also exceptions. The simple fact is, not every company is going to have the opportunity to achieve a positioning as robust and defensible as theirs. And even those that do will still have to cope with the corrosive effects of the IT infrastructure and the ever increasing rapidity of process emulation and homogenization. Even if a sustainable competitive advantage remains the *sine qua non* of outstanding profitability, an ability to adapt and respond will be an increasingly important component of long-run success.

Strategy today therefore requires a broader and more nuanced definition of competitive advantage, one that encompasses traditional *sustainable advantages* but that also includes more transient *leverageable advantages*. A leverageable advantage can be defined as a privileged market position that, however fleeting, provides a stepping stone to another privileged position.[8] Unlike a sustainable advantage, a leverageable advantage is a way station, not a destination. But like a sustainable advantage, a leverageable advantage is a manifestation of deep and disciplined strategic thinking. It's more than just a reaction to current events; it's a deliberate move that builds on the past and prepares for the future.

To see the power of leverageable advantage, consider the recent history of Apple Computer. Left for dead just a few years ago, Apple has survived as a profitable company in the cutthroat PC business by returning to its original sources of sustainable advantage: a flair for design, a tight integration between hardware and software, a strong and meaningful brand,

and an exuberant dedication to product innovation. At the same time, however, Apple has also used these and other advantages as leverageable advantages. Its design skills, its adroitness at combining hardware and software, and its appeal to trendsetters provided the platform for a successful leap from PCs to music players. Today, Apple's iPod holds the dominant share of the MP3 player market while also selling at a premium price—a desirable position for any product. But Apple didn't stop there. Its privileged position in the MP3 hardware market, together with its stylish image and design aptitude, provided the leverage for a move into music retailing through the 2003 launch of its on-line iTunes Music Store. Although the store doesn't yet make a large profit itself, it has provided a further boost to lucrative iPod sales and reinforced Apple's brand. Going from selling computers to selling songs seems on the face of it an unlikely strategic shift. But for Apple it made sense—it had the logic of leverageable advantage.[9]

The shared IT infrastructure will continue to dissolve operating advantages, particularly those based on the superior execution of an isolated, transaction-intensive process or activity. But more complex positioning advantages—those derived from broad and tightly integrated combinations of processes, capabilities, and, yes, technologies—will continue to resist rapid emulation. Successful companies will therefore work to establish and protect distinctive strategic positions even as they use more temporary competitive advantages as stepping stones to new advantages. They will be, so to speak, flexibly inflexible.

In Praise of Walls

In addition to homogenizing business practices, the new IT infrastructure can also dissolve existing advantages by blurring traditional organizational boundaries. Because computer networks, and the Internet in particular, make it easier for a company to coordinate work with other companies, they have led businesses to collaborate more intensively, sharing information about supply and demand, blending their processes, and outsourcing more and more activities. Such efforts can enhance industry productivity—again by removing the friction from business transactions—but they also have the potential to undermine a company's distinctiveness and hence, in the long run, its profitability. One of the central strategic challenges now facing managers is figuring out how to defend their companies' competitive advantages—many of which are built, in one way or another, on the proprietary control or distinctive use of information—while at the same time allowing information to flow freely in and out of their organizations through the general IT infrastructure.

One school of business experts—a very vocal one in recent years—turns a blind eye to this challenge. Citing the theoretical possibility of enormous efficiency gains from seamless collaboration, they argue that information porosity is entirely to the good. Indeed, they would have companies actively tear down the "walls" around their organizations and merge into great, amorphous "enterprise networks" or "business webs." One of most avid proponents of this concept, the Canadian business consultant Don Tapscott, has gone so far as to herald the death of the stand-alone company as the fundamental unit of commerce. In "Rethinking Strategy in a Networked World," an article written in response to Porter's "Strategy and the Internet," Tapscott argues that "in the future, strategists will no longer look at the integrated corporation as the starting point for creating value, assigning functions, and deciding what to manage inside or outside a firm's boundaries. Rather, strategists will start with a customer value proposition and a blank slate for the production and delivery system." Such an approach goes far beyond current conceptions of outsourcing, Tapscott stresses: "There will be nothing to 'outsource' because, from the point of view of strategy, there's nothing 'inside' to begin with."[10] Two other consultants, Larry Downes and Chunka Mui, put it more concisely in their bestselling book *Unleashing the Killer App*: "A truly frictionless economy needs no permanent firms."[11]

The post-company school has adopted the economist and Nobel laureate Ronald Coase as its high priest. In his brilliant 1937 essay "The Nature of the Firm," Coase explained why companies exist in the first place—why, in other words, it makes sense for some business activities to be coordinated by managers within a formal, hierarchical organization, rather than to be coordinated by the marketplace's invisible hand. "The significant question," as Coase put it, "would appear to be why the allocation of resources [within a company] is not done directly by the price mechanism [of an open market]."[12]

Coase's answer is that using a market entails various transaction costs over and above the actual price of a purchased good or service.[13] If a company decides to use an outside supplier to perform a particular activity, it has to search for and evaluate potential vendors, decide on terms and draw up contracts, collaborate in making decisions and fixing problems, monitor the supplier's performance, assume the risk of the supplier's failure, and so forth. But if it carries out that activity itself, using its own employees, it can often reduce or avoid these transaction costs. A company will, therefore, expand its organization to encompass any activity that it can carry out more cheaply than the total of the market price for performing the activity plus the attendant transaction costs. More generally, companies will tend to get bigger as external transaction costs increase and to shrink as they decrease.

The members of the post-company school, seeing that the Internet has reduced certain transaction costs, particularly those related to exchanging information, jump to the conclusion that companies will naturally get smaller. And then they make a further logical leap: As communication costs continue to fall and the integrative power of the Internet grows stronger, many business activities will eventually be able to be organized through markets, without any centralized control. Industries will begin to adopt the Hollywood model of production: Teams of specialists will come together to create a particular product or carry out some other business function and will then disassemble and reassemble in new ways, as market forces dictate. Managers and the companies they run will disappear entirely, as Bill Gates's vision of the Internet as "universal middleman" comes to fruition.

But this is a misreading of Coase.[14] It's true that the Internet reduces transaction costs within markets, but at the same time it reduces coordination costs within companies. In other words, it makes management itself more efficient, which can make it possible for even more activities to be incorporated economically within a single organization. Coase takes pains to point out the complex effects of innovations that influence transaction costs, writing that "most inventions will change both the costs of organising [within the firm] and the costs of using the price mechanism. In such cases, whether the invention tends to make firms larger or smaller will depend on the relative effect on these two sets of costs."[15] He then gets more specific, in a way that has a direct bearing on understanding the Internet's impact: "Changes like the telephone and telegraph which tend to reduce the cost of organizing spatially will tend to increase the size of the firm. All changes which improve managerial technique will tend to increase the size of the firm."[16]

History eloquently underscores Coase's point. Earlier infrastructural technologies that reduced communication and coordination costs—not just the telegraph and telephone but also the railroad and the automobile—did not lead to smaller firms. Just the opposite, in fact: They brought into being giant, vertically integrated companies. They made the complex modern business organization possible. It is dangerous to assume that the "death of distance," to borrow Frances Cairncross's description of the effect of new communication technologies, will mean the death of the company. In some cases, the Internet will lead business organizations to shrink by making it economical to outsource more work. In other cases, it will lead them to expand by bringing more work inside.

One professor of IT management, Harvard's Andrew McAfee, has even suggested that information technology may *increase* the relative cost of using the market to coordinate work. In the future, he argues, efficiency gains will hinge on the coordination of complex, highly automated vertical processes, such as the management of a supply chain or a distribution system. That coordination in turn hinges on the rigid standardization of processes, data, and information systems. It is often much easier, McAfee points out, for centralized management to impose such standardization on an organization than to wait for it to emerge organically through the complex and often conflicting interactions of free agents in a marketplace. Hierarchies, in other words, may outperform markets when it comes to integrating complex information systems, leading to a reemergence of the vertically integrated company.[17]

But beyond the practical economics, there can be important strategic reasons to keep diverse activities under the direct control of management. Any outside contractor will have its own economic incentives, which may or may not coincide with those of the company that hires it. It's fine to talk about "win-win partnerships" and "enlarging the pie," but in the end all companies in an industry are in competition to seize larger shares of the industry's profits for themselves. When a contractor's economic interests diverge from those of the company that hired it, the contractor can be expected to act in ways that bring harm to its partner. As the Berkeley economist Hal Varian wrote in a perceptive article about Coase's ideas, "If certain suppliers are critical to your success, you want them inside, under your control, not outside, where their objectives may differ from yours."[18] Even when it costs less to outsource an activity, you might not want to do it—the strategic risks may outweigh the cost savings.

What's truly dangerous about the post-company school's argument is its obliviousness to the competitive realities of business. By shifting the focus away from the productivity and profitability of individual firms and toward the productivity and profitability of loose groupings of firms, post-company pundits encourage managers to act in ways that may in the long run erode their own companies' advantages and financial results. They would have companies turn themselves into highly specialized modules in broad "plug-and-play" business networks. As Richard Veryard puts it in his book *The Component-Based Business,* "Thanks to the plug-and-play approach, a new business can be rapidly assembled as a loosely coupled set of partnerships and services. . . . Even a substantial company can now be viewed as a component of a much larger system, rather than as a self-contained business operation."[19]

Such a view reveals a common shortcoming in the thinking of technologists: their tendency to confuse business with information processing, to want to see companies as, in essence, computers. They overlook, or give short shrift to, the physical and human characteristics of commercial organizations—to all the things that can't be reduced to digital code, that can't be "exposed" or "made transparent" through networks. This skewed perception leads them to conclude that companies, like computers, can and should become components, or modules, in broad and flexible networks.[20] But as the history of the IT infrastructure itself shows, becoming a standardized module often means becoming a commodity—what can be easily plugged in can just as easily be unplugged. In the end, standardized, modular companies would have fewer ways to distinguish themselves; the evaluation of their performance would be reduced to a few easily compared measures. In many cases, that would leave only one basis for competition: the price at which they can carry out their specialized function. For many companies, participation in a seamless "business web" would virtually guarantee an existence unleavened by profit.

That's not to say that a company should pull back into its shell. Figuring out how broad or narrow a role to play in an industry value chain has always been, and will always be, a central strategic decision. It's simply to say that, in assessing potential partnerships or outsourcing opportunities, managers should be careful to keep their own company's interests foremost. Smart companies will resist knee-jerk specialization and modularization, recognizing that they may undermine the complex advantages on which true long-term success is founded. Instead, wise companies will use the IT infrastructure to establish business relationships that enhance, rather than diminish, their own economic and strategic power, while also providing meaningful incentives for their partners.

JPMorgan Chase has done precisely that in the automotive finance business. It joined with Americredit and Wells Fargo to launch an on-line system, called DealerTrack, that allows car dealers to automate loan origination and processing. But JPMorgan was not simply looking to increase general industry productivity; it was using the shared IT infrastructure to enhance its market power. It knew that its existing large-scale lending operation gave it a cost advantage over the other lenders that would use the DealerTrack system, so it was confident that it would be able to undercut the competition in pricing loans. By automating the search for loans and the comparison of their terms, DealerTrack simply made it easier for more dealers to discover JPMorgan's superior pricing, making the company's existing cost advantage all the more powerful.[21] Its partners win, but it wins more.

The universal IT infrastructure creates pressure to homogenize business processes and organizations, and it may lead the unwary company into partnerships, outsourcing contracts, and specialization initiatives that foreclose opportunities for advantage and undermine long-run profitability. The thoughtful executive will resist the pressure, not give in to it. As ever, the worst thing a business leader can do is to go with the flow.

The Need for Bifocal Vision

The philosophers of business strategy have long been organized into two loose camps. There are the classicists who take an "industry-based view," believing that a successful strategy hinges on a clear understanding of an industry's economic and competitive structure. The challenge for a company's leaders is to position their firm in such a way that it is able to capture the largest possible share of industry profits. Strategy making, for the classicists, begins by looking outside. And then there are the scholars who take a "resource-based view" of strategy. To them, the essence of strategy lies not outside the firm but within it—in a company's distinctive resources or capabilities. The challenge for a company's executives is to figure out what the company does best and then turn that "core competency" into an advantage over the competition. Strategy making, in this view, begins by looking inside.

The most successful business executives ignore such academic distinctions, of course. They realize, intuitively, that successful strategy is about *both* achieving a privileged industry position *and* exploiting unique internal capabilities. They know, in other words, that business success derives from a continuous and purposeful mediation between what lies inside and what lies outside. The maturation of the IT infrastructure, with its corrosive effects on competitive advantage, demands more such acts of practical synthesis. It requires that managers see a competitive advantage as both a goal and a passageway, an end and a means. And it requires that they defend their company's integrity as a stand-alone business even as they exploit the tighter connections to other companies made possible by computer networks. Agility must be balanced with stability, openness with guardedness. Those executives who are able to master such bifocal vision without losing their ability to take forceful action will be the ones that build the great and lasting companies of the twenty-first century.

CHAPTER 6

Managing the Money Pit

New Imperatives for IT
Investment and Management

IN THE SUMMER of 1997, the U.S. railroad system broke down. As the recently merged Union Pacific and Southern Pacific struggled vainly to combine their operations, their vast rail network became gridlocked, and thousands of cargo shipments were delayed, misrouted, or lost. On October 31, the federal government stepped in, declaring a transportation emergency throughout much of the country. Particularly hard hit were industrial and agricultural companies in Texas, many of which were served solely by Union Pacific lines. By early 1998, for example, the U.S. arm of the large Mexican cement producer Cemex had seen outbound rail service at its Texas plants cut by 50 percent, and the company was losing hundreds of thousands of dollars worth of sales every month. Gulf Coast chemical companies incurred an estimated half billion dollars in extra costs as they were forced to curtail production and switch to more expensive modes of transport.[1]

Many companies in California endured a similarly unpleasant experience three years later. The culprit this time wasn't the rail system but the electric grid. When a misguided regulatory regime, combined with rash speculation, created an electricity shortage in the state, prices skyrocketed and utilities were forced to impose rolling blackouts to reduce demand. The resulting disruptions cost California companies hundreds of millions of dollars and forced some manufacturers to shut down their operations altogether. In a speech at the time, Intel CEO Craig Barrett vented the frustration of the business community, calling California a "Third World country" and threatening to stop building new plants in the state.[2]

The companies affected by these two debacles were blindsided by the events. Having come to take rail and electric service for granted, they had few contingency plans in place. They found themselves at the mercy of a technology infrastructure that their operations depended on but over which they had little control. Their experience underscores what is perhaps the most important managerial lesson to be learned from the pattern of evolution of infrastructural technologies: When a resource becomes essential to competition but inconsequential to strategy, the risks it creates become more important than the advantages it provides. Today, no company builds its business strategy around rail service or electricity, but a lapse in the supply of these resources, or a spike in their cost, can be devastating.

Fortunately, the risks associated with infrastructural technologies diminish as the technologies mature and become more stable and resilient. Rail and electricity disruptions, once common, have become rare occurrences in the developed world (although the blackouts in North America and Italy in 2003 underscore the dangers of taking established infrastructures for granted). But earlier in their progress, particularly during and immediately after their buildout, infrastructural technologies present grave business risks. It's easy to see why. When it becomes clear that a new business infrastructure is emerging, companies invest heavily in the underlying technology, incorporating it into many aspects of their operations and often making substantial alterations to their processes and organizations. They have little choice but to act; adapting to the new infrastructure is for most companies a competitive necessity. Yet because the technology is new, it is unstable, untested, and prone to disruption, which can wreak havoc on a company's operations. Executives, moreover, have relatively little knowledge of and experience with the technology—the best ways to evaluate investments and manage assets are not yet clear—and as a result they often make the wrong choices in buying and using it. In other words, companies are forced to install a critical new business resource before they've learned how to manage it effectively.

That's certainly been true of information technology. Although industry as a whole has made great progress in adopting IT, a different picture emerges when you look at individual firms. As companies have installed systems during the IT buildout, they've made many missteps and wrong turns. Some of the biggest fiascos have been widely publicized.[3] Oxford Health Plans' market capitalization fell by $3 billion in a single day after it announced that software problems had led to widespread errors in billing and claims processing. Nike's difficulties in installing supply-chain software cost it an estimated $400 million. Delays in the rollout of a new ordering system at tool manufacturer Snap-on led to a 40 percent dip in earnings. A disastrous implementation of an ERP system helped push FoxMeyer Drug into bankruptcy. A new $9 million logistics system at W.W. Grainger miscounted inventory, leading to a profit drop of $23 million. Cigna lost 6 percent of its health care accounts after a flawed installation of a customer relationship management system. Cisco System's much-vaunted "real time" forecasting system failed to spot an imminent freefall in demand for networking equipment, leading to a $2.5 billion inventory write-down and the firing of 8,500 workers. Even the operational meltdown that followed the Southern Pacific–Union Pacific merger can be traced largely to the companies' inability to coordinate their IT systems.

Nearly every sizable company has its own horror stories about IT projects that went wildly over budget or off schedule, that never came close to delivering the promised benefits, or that were simply abandoned. A study conducted by the Standish Group in 1995 uncovered a striking record of failure in IT projects.[4] Of the more than eight thousand systems projects Standish examined, only 16 percent were considered successes—completed on time and on budget and fulfilling the original specifications. Nearly a third were canceled outright, and the remainder all went over budget, off schedule, and out-of-spec. Large companies—those with more than $500 million in annual sales—did even worse than the average: Only 9 percent of their IT projects succeeded.

And when IT projects fail, Standish found, they fail in a big way. Most of the cost overruns amounted to more than 50 percent of the original budget, and nearly a quarter of the over-budget projects exceeded estimated costs by 100 percent or more. Of the projects that went off schedule, 48 percent took more than twice as long as originally planned, and 12 percent took at least three times as long. Of the projects that were completed but fell short of initial expectations, more than 30 percent failed to deliver even half of the originally specified features and functions. Standish also found that almost all the projects—94 percent—had to be restarted at some point, and some had to be restarted several times over.

In a follow-up survey in 1998, Standish found some improvement, but the overall picture remained bleak. Although the percentage of successful projects had risen to 26 percent, this was still less than the percentage that had been canceled (28 percent) or that failed to achieve their intended results (46 percent).[5] Another 1998 study, by accountants KPMG, delivered even worse news. Of the 1,450 companies surveyed, three-quarters said that their IT projects exceeded their deadlines and more than half said that the projects went substantially over budget. When KPMG analyzed 100 of the failed initiatives, it found that 87 percent of them had gone over budget by more than 50 percent.[6] Bob Napier, the chief technology officer of Hewlett-Packard, summed up the situation well in a 2003 interview: "The number of projects that fail is scary."[7]

Many of the failures were, in retrospect, inevitable, a natural consequence of the process of trial and error that goes on as any new technology is adopted by business. Trying to place blame on any one group—vendors, consultants, CEOs, CIOs—would at this point be a futile exercise. The challenge now is to bring the failure rate down—quickly and sharply. Given the high risks inherent in IT projects and the declining likelihood that they will lead to the durable advantages necessary for higher profits, both users and vendors need to concentrate on such mundane but essential requirements as efficiency, predictability, reliability, and security. The time has come, in other words, for a more conservative approach to IT management. As the infrastructure matures, the companies that succeed will not be those that reflexively pursue innovation, that seek to push the proverbial envelope, but rather those that are pragmatic in planning and competent in execution.

Spend Less

IT management presents companies with many risks, but at the moment the greatest of them all is overspending. Information technology may be a commodity, and its costs may fall rapidly enough to ensure that any new capabilities are quickly shared, but the very fact that it is entwined with so many business functions means that it will go on consuming a large portion of corporate spending for the foreseeable future. Information technology will continue to be "an insatiable economic sump," as author James McKenney memorably described computing during the mainframe era.[8] What's important—and this holds true for any commodity input—is to be able to separate essential investments and activities from ones that are discretionary, unnecessary, or even counterproductive.

The first challenge facing managers is to put their IT house in order. Most companies can reap significant savings by simply cutting out waste. Personal computers provide a good example. Businesses purchase more than one hundred million PCs every year, most of which replace older models. Yet the vast majority of workers who use PCs rely on only a few simple applications—word processing, spreadsheets, e-mail, and Web browsing. These applications have been technologically mature for years; they require only a fraction of the computing power provided by today's microprocessors. Nevertheless, companies have continued to roll out across-the-board hardware and software upgrades, often every two or three years.

Much of the spending, if truth be told, is driven not by the interests of the buyers but by the strategies of the sellers. Big hardware and software suppliers have become very good at parceling out new features and capabilities in ways that force companies to buy new computers and applications much more frequently than they need to. Intel and Microsoft, in particular, have created a very lucrative cycle of releasing faster microprocessors and more complex software; buying one often leaves companies with no choice but to upgrade the other. Some vendors of expensive enterprise systems such as ERP software even require clients to upgrade to new versions in order to continue to receive maintenance. Since vendor support is critical to keeping the complex systems running, businesses have little choice but to pay the tab.

But if there's a silver lining in the commoditization of IT, it's that the balance of power is tipping away from the vendor and toward the user. With competition among suppliers intensifying, IT buyers are now in a position to throw their weight around much more aggressively—negotiating contracts, for example, that ensure the long-term viability of their PC investments, tie payments to actual usage, incorporate tough service-level agreements, and impose hard limits on upgrade costs. And if vendors balk, companies should be willing to explore cheaper solutions, including open-source applications and barebones network PCs, even if it means sacrificing features. If a company needs evidence of the kind of money that might be saved, it need only look at Microsoft's huge profit margins on PC software.

But PCs are just one example. Wasteful IT spending has long been endemic in corporations, and it reached plague-like proportions during the Internet boom of the late 1990s, when, as one computer industry executive put it, "servers were growing like bacteria." [9] Today, in the wake of all the excess spending, "considerably less than half of [installed] IT capacity is actually used," reports the *Financial Times*. [10] Needless to say, much of the superfluous hardware and software will never be used—it's already out of date. But the lesson is clear:

Companies need to make sure they get the value out of past investments before making new ones.

Businesses also have opportunities to impose tighter controls on IT usage. That's particularly true with data storage, which has come to account for more than half of many firms' capital spending on IT.[11] The bulk of what's being stored on corporate networks has little to do with making products or serving customers—it consists of employees' saved e-mails and files, including terabytes worth of spam, MP3s, and video clips. *Computerworld* estimates that as much of 70 percent of the storage capacity of a typical Windows network is being wasted—an enormous unnecessary expense.[12] Restricting employees' ability to save files indiscriminately and indefinitely may seem distasteful to many managers, but even such a simple step can have a real impact on the bottom line. Now that IT has become the dominant capital expense for most businesses, there's no excuse for waste and sloppiness.

One business that is moving to exert tighter control over its network is the hotel-franchising unit of Cendant. It realized that the thousands of reservations agents who book rooms for its properties were wasting time surfing the Web and downloading games and other personal applications and files from the Internet. Seeing that there was no business benefit to giving agents access to the Web, the unit's IT director, David Chugg, decided to simply remove the browser application from the agents' PCs. But that turned out to be impossible, since Microsoft has integrated its Explorer browser with its Windows operating system. So Chugg took the radical step of replacing the existing Windows machines with desktops running a version of the Linux operating system. He's glad he did. Not only has the company increased its agents' productivity and cleaned up its network, it has cut its software licensing costs significantly.[13]

At a higher level, stronger cost management requires more rigor in systems planning and assessment and more creativity in exploring simpler and cheaper hardware, software, and service alternatives. A handful of companies are showing just how much money can be saved by taking a systematic approach to cost containment. General Electric is one. GE spends some $3.3 billion a year on IT—equal to about half the gross national product of Ethiopia—yet its chief information officer, Gary Reiner, is not above browsing eBay auctions to look for good buys on used gear. Through a concerted and multifaceted effort to reduce costs—shifting corporate applications to cheap Linux servers, leveraging the fiber-optic glut to negotiate much lower rates for data transmission, using low-cost Indian labor for software development, and so on—Reiner succeeded in cutting GE's IT budget from 2.8 percent of revenues in 2000 to 2.5 percent in 2002.[14]

General Motors' CIO Ralph Szygenda has also been relentless in trimming the automaker's vast IT expenditures. After telling some of his top lieutenants that they each had to cut $100 million from their annual budgets, he came back and ordered them to chop $50 million more. In addition to disconnecting many underperforming systems and consolidating others, Szygenda has increasingly unloaded IT work to outside contractors. By the end of 2002, GM was no longer employing any in-house programmers—all the work had been outsourced. Most of the company's remaining 1,800 IT staffers are dedicated to riding herd on contractors and vendors, monitoring the quality of their work and negotiating the cheapest possible prices on equipment and services. Szygenda's approach has paid off for GM. In his first six years on the job, he has slashed the company's annual IT spending by $800 million.[15] GM's competitors have followed suit. Between 2002 and 2003, Ford cut its yearly IT budget by $300 million, or 20 percent. DaimlerChrysler cut its systems costs for crash testing by 40 percent—and improved performance by 20 percent—by replacing three mainframes with a hundred commodity servers.

Even companies whose entire business is built on the IT infrastructure have managed to trim their expenditures substantially. Verizon's CIO, Shaygan Kheradpir, cut the telecommunications company's IT spending from 6 percent of sales—the average for companies in its industry—to 4 percent between 2001 and 2003. Some of the savings came from staffing cuts, as he reduced IT labor by 20 percent, but much has come through tough bargaining with vendors. In early 2002, Kheradpir put a moratorium on all new computer purchases. Then he went to the company's three main server suppliers—Sun, Hewlett-Packard, and IBM—and told them that their share of Verizon's future purchases would be determined solely by the prices they charged. The vendors all cut their prices by 25 percent, and Sun and HP offered deep reductions in maintenance fees as well.

Capitalizing on the commoditization of hardware, Kheradpir has also pushed other vendors for concessions. Like GE's Reiner, he routinely scans eBay's prices for used storage equipment, and he then has his purchasing agents use that information as a bargaining chip in negotiating prices for new gear from their main storage supplier, EMC. And he has demanded that EMC and other vendors provide Verizon with "capacity on demand," charging only for the storage and processing capacity that the company actually uses, regardless of how much is installed. Verizon is also saving about $50 million a year by shifting contract development work from the United States to India. The company has found that using Indian labor not only reduces the cost of writing software but also significantly quickens its pace, as the time difference between India and the United States enables programming to proceed around the clock. When Verizon's in-house programmers get to work in the morning, they have clean code from India to work on.[16]

E-Trade, the big Internet broker, has dramatically cut the cost of its most critical IT asset, its on-line trading system. Back in 1998, the company spent more than $14 million to buy sixty Sun servers, while also agreeing to pay Sun $1.5 million in annual maintenance fees. In 2002, however, E-Trade replaced the Sun machines with eighty Linux servers costing just $4,000 apiece, or $320,000 in all. The changeover also brought a dramatic reduction in maintenance costs. E-Trade CIO Josh Levine has expressed relief at being freed from proprietary systems. "We get to manage the vendor as opposed to the vendor managing us," he told *CIO* magazine.[17]

Because of the rapidly increasing power and capabilities of commodity hardware and software, it's often possible for companies to make dramatic cost reductions in a relatively short span of time, with little disruption to their business. Amazon.com, for instance, was able to shift more than 90 percent of its servers from proprietary Unix systems, such as Sun's Solaris and Compaq's Tru64, to the open-source Linux system in just three months, cutting $17 million from its quarterly IT budget in the process. The only servers still running proprietary systems are the ones in Amazon's corporate data center, which house the all-important pricing and customer data for the company's on-line store. And Amazon is looking to shift even these mission-critical machines to Linux. "We are not prepared to stop here," the company's director of systems engineering said in a speech at the 2002 LinuxWorld conference. "Our goal is really to do an end-to-end migration to Linux."[18]

None of these companies is cutting costs blindly or reactively. They are just capitalizing on the commoditization of IT, shifting to the cheaper systems and lower-cost labor made possible by the increasing standardization and homogenization of the infrastructure. And when it makes sense to spend more in a particular area, they spend more. Verizon's Kheradpir, for instance, has aggressively upgraded the PCs used in the company's call centers in order to install faster versions of the complex software that the customer service representatives use. By reducing call times, the faster processors improve the centers' overall productivity as well as enhancing customer service. For the other PCs used in the company, however,

Kheradpir has slowed the upgrade cycle. He'll bring in new machines only when the economic benefits are clear and compelling.

The commoditization of IT will continue to give companies new opportunities for reducing costs and risks. Price comparisons, for example, are becoming easier as the basis for vendor competition continues to shift to costs. In a telling 2003 move, Sun Microsystems adopted a standardized pricing model for enterprise software, announcing that it would start charging companies a flat fee of $100 per employee per year, covering not only a comprehensive array of networking software but also support and training. Commoditization is coming to IT services as well, as indicated by the rapid expansion of service outsourcers in India and other developing countries. In describing his own company's intention to drive down the costs of IT services, Michael Dell told the *Financial Times,* "The fact is that you can put some mystical notion on lots of these services, but if you look at them in detail, look at what's really going on, you'll find that many of the things that [service professionals] are doing are highly repeatable. . . . We are in effect commoditizing services. There is no reason why this can't occur."[19] The ability to understand and capitalize on such trends will be a hallmark of effective IT management for many years to come.

Follow, Don't Lead

It's not always necessary to make outright cuts to save considerable sums of cash. One powerful way to reduce costs without forgoing new systems is simply to spend more slowly. The rapid, ongoing fall in IT prices means that even small delays in purchases can dramatically reduce the cost of achieving a given level of IT functionality. And delaying IT investments can have other beneficial effects as well. Companies that stay off the leading edge reduce their chance of being saddled with buggy or soon-to-be-obsolete technology. They are also able to learn from the successes and mistakes of early movers, enabling them not only to avoid unnecessary costs but, often, to build better systems as well.

Many companies have rushed their IT investments, out of either a hope of capturing a first-mover advantage or a fear of being left behind. That was particularly true in the late 1990s, when the Internet boom coincided with "Y2K" fears and the introduction of the euro. Business magazines produced a steady stream of articles urging executives to install the latest systems or risk being consigned to the dustbin of business history, a theme echoed by IT vendors and consultants. As late as February 2001, Cisco CEO John Chambers was telling an audience of corporate IT managers that "the Internet changes everything: every company in the world is in a period of transition. There will be no company except an e-business company ten years from now." Executives "need to think about technology changes as waves," he went on. "The leaders will always be one or two waves ahead in applications or services and the laggards one or two waves behind."[20] At that same event, a senior partner at the consultancy Pricewaterhouse-Coopers was even more emphatic, telling companies that "the game is changing and they need to make abrupt and accurate changes or they will lose; and they will lose big. . . . [T]here is no fast-follower strategy."[21]

Such rhetoric made for good marketing, but it was largely hollow. Except in rare cases, both the hope of achieving a defensible advantage through IT spending and the fear of obsolescence from failing to invest turned out to be unwarranted. It has become increasingly clear that many of the smartest users of technology stay well back from the cutting edge, waiting to make their purchases until standards and best practices solidify and prices fall. They let their more impatient competitors shoulder the high costs of experimentation, and then they sweep past them, spending less and getting more.

Look at the package delivery business. FedEx has received widespread, and well-deserved, acclaim for its efforts at pioneering new IT applications, such as on-line package tracking. Less appreciated has been the more deliberate approach taken by its archrival, UPS. In fact, UPS was often attacked through the 1980s and 1990s for being a technological slow-poke. All the while, though, UPS was carefully following in FedEx's tracks, learning not just how to copy its rival's systems but often how to make them better and cheaper. When UPS rolled out its own logistics-management software, for instance, it went with a more open system than FedEx's, making it easier for customers to incorporate UPS's technology into their existing systems.

Far from hampering UPS, the slow, copycat approach paid off. By the late 1990s, some big shippers had begun to shift their logistics contracts from FedEx to UPS. National Semiconductor, for one, abandoned a Singapore warehouse constructed by FedEx in favor of a new, more flexible one operated by UPS.[22] Today, ironically, UPS handles far more shipments from Internet retailers than its more technologically aggressive rival, and it remains more profitable as well. When it comes to IT, the tortoise often beats the hare.

Some managers may fear that being stingy with IT dollars will damage their competitive positions. But they need not worry. Studies of corporate IT spending consistently show that greater expenditures rarely translate into superior financial results. In fact, the opposite is as likely to be true. In 2002, the consulting firm Alinean compared the IT expenditures and financial results of 7,500 large U.S. companies and found that the top performers tended to be among the most tight-fisted spenders. The twenty-five companies that delivered the highest economic returns, for example, spent on average just 0.8 percent of their revenues on IT, while the twenty-five worst performers spent 2.7 percent and the average company spent 3.7 percent. Another measure—IT spending per employee—showed a similar pattern. The best performers spent just $3,903 for each employee, while the worst performers spent $6,250 and the average company spent $10,283.[23]

Another recent study, by Forrester Research, also found no connection between IT spending and business results. Forrester examined 291 companies, comparing their IT spending as a percentage of revenues with their financial performance over a three-year period, as measured by revenue growth, return on assets, and cash-flow growth. It found that while the worst-performing companies spent the least on IT (2.6 percent of sales), the best performers spent the second least (3.3 percent). The biggest spenders (4.4 percent) turned in middling results.[24]

One of the largest studies of the impact of information technology on business performance was carried out by the McKinsey Global Institute, the internal think tank of the management consultancy McKinsey & Company. In a three-year study, the institute examined IT spending and business productivity at the industry and firm levels in the United States, Germany, and France. It, too, found "no correlation" between IT investment and performance. The real driver of business productivity improvements during the 1990s, the study discovered, was competition, which pushed managers to take aggressive measures to improve their companies' efficiency and effectiveness. In those industries with the strongest competitive pressures, IT investments produced positive returns. But where competition was more restrained, even the most aggressive IT spending had little benefit.[25]

Extensive studies undertaken by Paul Strassman, one of the elder statesmen of IT management, back up these findings. Strassman, who has served as the CIO of Kraft, Xerox, and NASA, has been researching the link between IT spending and business results for more than twenty years. His studies, including a 2001 analysis of 1,585 U.S. firms, have also revealed absolutely no correlation between how much a company spends on IT and how well it performs. "The relationship between profits and IT is random," Strassman told the *Financial Times* in late 2001. "From now on, it's economics—and the role of the CIO is to make money. Technology has to be taken for granted."[26] Even Oracle's Larry Ellison, one of the great technology salesmen of all time, admitted in a 2002 interview that "most companies spend too much [on IT] and get very little in return." [27]

Many firms have become accustomed to double-digit increases in their annual IT budgets. They consider it a victory if they're able just to cut the rate of increase in spending. But a very different approach may now be in order. As the opportunities for IT-based advantage continue to diminish, the penalties for overspending will only grow. Following the lead of GM, Verizon, and the other companies that have actually reduced their year-over-year IT spending, more businesses may want to establish explicit goals for trimming their IT budgets—by 5 percent a year, say. That won't be the right target for every company, of course. Some may find it makes good business sense to invest more heavily in IT in the short run—in order, for example, to replace outdated systems with new ones that offer more efficiency and flexibility—and others may need to increase their spending simply to maintain their competitiveness. But why not start with the assumption that IT spending should now go down every year, not up, and then make exceptions as the business requires?

Innovate When Risks Are Low

Although most companies will find that the risks of aggressive IT innovation now outweigh the potential benefits, there are still times when it makes strategic sense to get out ahead of the competition. Companies should, in general, look for situations in which they can reduce or avoid the high costs associated with being a first mover or in which their competitors face barriers to rapidly copying IT innovations. Where risk can be tempered, innovation can pay off.

Large companies with substantial market power, for example, may have opportunities to use infrastructural innovations to fortify their existing advantages. A good example is Wal-Mart's early move to promote the adoption of radio frequency identification in the consumer packaged goods sector. RFID, as it's usually called, involves "tagging" products with tiny chips and transmitters that allow the goods to be identified and tracked throughout their journey along the supply chain, from the time they are manufactured to the time they are sold (and even beyond, in some cases). Because RFID provides companies with more precise control over inventory, it promises to boost overall industry productivity.

In 2003, Wal-Mart announced that it would require its one hundred largest suppliers to place RFID tags on the boxes and pallets they ship to the retailer by January 2005. Because of Wal-Mart's dominance as a retailer, its move increases the odds that RFID technology will become an industry standard, in much the same way barcoding did in the 1970s. In effect, Wal-Mart is pushing to quickly turn RFID technology into a commodity, a part of the infrastructure used by all consumer goods manufacturers and retailers. Its move makes strategic sense for two reasons. First, by commoditizing a powerful new technology, Wal-Mart neutralizes it as a potential strategic weapon for its competitors; its rivals end up with even less room to maneuver. Second, because Wal-Mart is the scale and cost leader in consumer goods retailing, it stands to reap a disproportionate share of any general productivity gains in the industry.

But here's the real kicker: Although Wal-Mart is making substantial investments in RFID, most of the costs of adopting the new technology will end up falling on the shoulders of its suppliers. According to a study by AMR Research, manufacturers will have to spend some $2 billion just to comply with the Wal-Mart mandate.[28] "Right now, the benefits are primarily for Wal-Mart, and the costs are the responsibility of the suppliers," observed an AMR researcher.[29] By pushing the costs onto others, Wal-Mart stands to reap the gains of being a first mover without incurring the risks. It's using its enormous market power to put itself in a no-lose situation.

Companies can also reduce risk by pursuing innovations that competitors would have a hard time adopting. In most cases, these will involve narrow and highly specialized applications of IT—ones that are resistant to widespread adoption, rapid standardization, and diffusion through vendors.[30] A manufacturer that has outstanding capabilities in factory automation, for instance, may be able to further its lead by pioneering cutting-edge robotics control systems. Competitors may be unable to adopt similar systems without overhauling their current processes and plants. By pursuing incremental innovations tightly tied to its existing operations, a company can in effect slow down the technology replication cycle.

Sometimes, start-ups and other small companies will have relatively low-risk opportunities to capitalize on the new IT infrastructure to gain an edge on industry leaders. In businesses that involve complicated and idiosyncratic operations, for example, traditional competitors typically have highly complex, proprietary information systems in place. It can be difficult, if not impossible, for these companies to quickly replace those systems with new ones—the costs and disruptions would simply be too severe. Their inability to rapidly realize the benefits of advances in the IT infrastructure provides a competitive opening to newcomers.

The airline industry is a perfect example. The massive IT investments that big carriers have made to help them manage reservations, pricing, flight scheduling, crew assignments, maintenance, and so on, have locked them into particular modes of operation. And given their necessarily low tolerance for errors and other disruptions—not to mention their regulatory, labor, and financial constraints—changing those systems and processes would take a long time. That fact has allowed new carriers to pioneer IT applications with the knowledge that the industry leaders will be unlikely to mimic the innovations quickly. Look at New York–based JetBlue, for example. It has built its systems to realize the efficiencies provided by today's increasingly open and shared IT infrastructure. Its pilots use laptops rather than paper to track flight plans and other critical information. Its reservation agents work at home on PCs, taking calls over the Internet rather than the more expensive traditional phone network. There's nothing particularly radical about JetBlue's technologies; they are all widely available, affordable, and fairly easy to implement. They're strategically meaningful to JetBlue only because its competitors' existing business models prevent them from rapidly adopting such innovations.

It's important to keep the successes of companies like Jet-Blue in perspective. They are often used as examples of the "strategic power" of IT. But it's not that simple. Although Jet-Blue's IT initiatives support its competitive advantage, the source of that advantage lies not in the technology but in the business model, particularly the newness and relative simplicity of the airline's operations. As of early 2004 JetBlue was flying about fifty planes, all of the same type, to fewer than twenty-five cities, all in the United States. American Airlines, one of its big competitors, was serving some 150 cities around the world with a diverse fleet of 840 planes. JetBlue had fewer than 10,000 employees; American had more than 112,000. American's labor force is unionized; JetBlue's is not. The fact is, more complex operations require more complex information systems—a point too often overlooked when comparing the performance of different companies. And when scale economies are as constrained as they are in the airline business—adding flights means buying more planes and fuel and hiring more air and ground crews—the cost of complexity becomes particularly onerous. In general, we're too quick to attribute business advantages to the technology and too slow to attribute technology advantages to the business. That bias is one reason that the potential for IT-based advantages continues to be overstated.

When discussing IT innovation, it's also critical to note the importance of joint efforts. Although it makes sense for most individual companies to adopt a conservative approach to IT investment, it can be dangerous for an entire region or industry to put the brakes on innovation, particularly when the innovation will make the general IT infrastructure more secure, reliable, and efficient. In time, the slow-moving region or industry could put itself at a competitive disadvantage to other regions and industries. Often, competition among vendors will itself ensure that infrastructural advances continue, but that may not always be the case. It would be wise, therefore, for companies to think not only of their own strategic interests but of the broader interests of their region and industry. In particular, groups of companies may want to work together to make improvements to the IT infrastructure that will benefit them all. Spreading the costs and other risks of IT innovation makes sense when the innovation is unlikely to provide any one company with an advantage.

Focus More on Vulnerabilities than Opportunities

Overspending may be the greatest immediate risk related to the IT infrastructure, but it is far from the only one. IT presents many operational dangers—technical glitches, obsolescence, service outages, unreliable vendors or partners, worms and viruses, security breaches, spam, disclosure of confidential data, denial-of-service attacks, even terrorism—and some have become magnified as companies have moved from tightly controlled, proprietary systems to open, shared ones. As corporate systems have become accessible through the Internet, for example, attacks on Web sites and networks have proliferated. Today, it's estimated that nine out of ten companies experience unauthorized intrusions into their networks every year, with the total cost of the resulting damage running to $17 billion annually. Even the relatively benign Code Red worm, which infected thousands of corporate servers running Microsoft Windows in 2001, cost companies around the world some $2.6 billion.[31]

IT disruptions are not only costly; they can paralyze a company's ability to make its products, deliver its services, and connect with its customers, not to mention fouling its reputation. Yet few companies have done a thorough job of identifying and tempering their vulnerabilities. While no business can take all the risks out of computing, some basic steps can help reduce the dangers and stem the potential damage. First and perhaps most important, there needs to be somebody responsible for the integrity of a company's systems. Security doesn't happen on its own. Large companies may want to appoint a full-time IT security executive; smaller companies may want to explicitly incorporate security into the responsibilities of an existing business or technology executive, perhaps even the chief financial officer. Second, companies need to meticulously itemize and prioritize their IT risks through, for example, regular security audits. They need to look at threats not only from outside their corporate firewall but also from inside, since many IT disruptions originate with vindictive or careless employees. Third, an integrated risk-abatement program involving in-house staff, IT vendors, security contractors, and insurers needs to be established and carried out, with particular emphasis on educating all employees about IT vulnerabilities and laying out their specific responsibilities. Finally, companies need to elevate the importance—and the rewards—of maintaining secure systems. Worrying about what might go wrong may not be as glamorous a job as speculating about future IT advances, but it is a more essential job right now.

Reducing vulnerabilities often has important organizational implications. Today, many companies continue to allow individual business units considerable freedom in selecting and managing their own hardware and software and hiring their own IT staffs. Such a decentralized approach can have important benefits, strengthening the businesses' responsiveness to their markets and keeping corporate bureaucracy in check. But it can bring considerable risks as well—increasing the odds of incompatible systems, reducing purchasing power, and weakening the security of the company's overall information systems. Although it would be an overstatement to suggest that all companies move to impose rigid, central control over their IT assets and people, it's clear that the risks of a decentralized approach are growing. Every company should take a hard look at its IT organization with a view to imposing tighter controls and oversight while remaining sensitive to the different needs of its business units. This is sure to be a contentious exercise, but the stakes are too high for it to be put off.

As companies move from buying and maintaining discrete pieces of hardware and software to managing a complex, integrated infrastructure, the importance of accomplished technical staff can't be overstated. While business executives need to assume direct responsibility for the efficiency, effectiveness, and security of their companies' IT assets, there's no getting around the fact that installing, maintaining, and protecting systems require deep and often arcane technical knowledge. Until now, senior executives have had a tendency to view IT workers as generic, interchangeable parts—as faceless technicians—rather than as unique individuals with widely varying aptitudes and backgrounds. That view needs to change. As companies shift their focus away from the strategic implications of hardware and software systems to the way those systems are employed, the skills of the IT staff become more, not less, important.

At the same time, the way IT specialists are deployed is likely to change dramatically. As control over the IT infrastructure continues to shift from users to vendors, more and more traditional IT jobs will be performed remotely, by contractors, and in-house IT departments will likely shrink. In additional to strong technical expertise, therefore, the remaining IT employees will need to become more deeply skilled in the arts of negotiation, in order to bargain effectively with suppliers, and of management, in order to coordinate the work of a heterogeneous and far-flung workforce. Today, there is probably no better way to reduce IT risk than to attract and retain the best IT talent.

As for the seniormost corporate IT executives—the chief information officers—they need to lead the way in promulgating a new sense of realism about the strengths and limitations of IT. Realism is particularly important in IT planning. The continuing assumption that IT has strategic value often leads to overoptimistic predictions of the returns from new investments, leading companies to spend too much too soon. When assessing spending proposals, it's not enough to run return-on-investment calculations. CIOs also need to lead the way in getting their organizations to think clearly about how competitors will respond and what those responses will mean for margins and profits. In particular, they need to take a hard look at whether projected cost savings or productivity gains will end up on their own company's bottom line or in the hands of customers. And they need to objectively assess whether any anticipated revenue gains are truly defensible.

CIOs' ultimate professional goal may well be to render themselves obsolete, to make the IT infrastructure so stable and robust, so taken for granted, that it no longer requires active high-level management. Max Hopper, the American Airlines executive who oversaw the Sabre system during the 1970s and went on to become the company's top IT manager, saw the writing on the wall back in 1990, when he bravely predicted that information systems would come to "be thought of more like electricity or the telephone network than as a decisive source of organizational advantage. In this world, a company trumpeting the appointment of a new chief information officer will seem as anachronistic as a company today naming a new vice president for water and gas. People like me will have succeeded when we have worked ourselves out of our jobs. Only then will our organizations be capable of embracing the true promise of information technology." [32] We're still a long way from fulfilling Hopper's vision, but getting there remains a worthy goal for IT executives.

As with any recipe for business success, the four guidelines laid out in this chapter—spend less; follow, don't lead; innovate when risks are low; and focus more on vulnerabilities than opportunities—should be viewed with a degree of suspicion. Every company will need to make its own choices based on an objective assessment of its particular challenges, circumstances, and needs. At certain points, it may make sense for a company to invest heavily in a particular IT system or capability or even to pursue a first-mover strategy. Most companies, however, would be best served by adopting the view that IT should be managed as a commodity input, not a strategic asset. The key to success for the vast majority of firms is no longer to seek advantage aggressively but to manage costs and risks meticulously. In the wake of the Internet bust, many executives have already begun to take a more conservative posture toward IT, spending more frugally and thinking more pragmatically. They're on the right course. The challenge will be to maintain that discipline as the business cycle strengthens and the chorus of hype about IT's strategic value rises anew.

7

A Dream of Wonderful Machines

The Reading, and Misreading, of Technological Change

J. LYONS & COMPANY'S decision to build the first business computer back in 1947 stands as one of the great acts of business innovation, a triumph of managerial foresight and ingenuity. And the decision paid off for the company, enabling it to automate labor-intensive business processes years ahead of its competitors. But for all its power and speed, the LEO computer could not save Lyons from obsolescence. The company's teashops, a staple of English life before the Second World War, slowly fell out of favor after the war as customers' tastes and routines shifted. The computer brought Lyons great operating benefits, but in the end, as one of the company's employees later recalled, it was "unable to arrest the decline of the teashops' popularity and therefore profitability." [1] In 1978, the company disappeared, swallowed up by a brewery.

In a retrospective interview with researchers from the London Science Museum, John Simmons, Lyons's executive director during the time LEO was designed and constructed, reminisced about the company's early hopes for computerization: "We dreamed of some wonderful machine where all you would need to do would be to feed in paper and press buttons and get all the answers you wanted; it was all very naïve." [2] The dream may have been naïve, but Lyons was neither the first nor the last company to dream it. The bewitchments of technology, particularly broadly adopted infrastructural technology, are hard to resist, and they go a long way toward explaining the outsized hopes that people have sometimes placed in computers.

Because it marks a break with the past, the arrival of any new infrastructural technology opens the future to speculation. It creates an intellectual clearing in which the imagination is free to play, unconstrained by old rules and experiences. Futurists spin elaborate scenarios of approaching paradises (or, less commonly, infernos), and every new vision of the future serves as a foundation for wilder conjecture. Hungry for spectacle, if only of the conceptual sort, the press rushes to promote each new theory, giving unwarranted credibility to even the most extravagant claims. Soon, the entire public becomes caught up in the excitement, sharing an intoxicating communal dream of renewal. The historian

David Nye describes this phenomenon—and its inevitable outcome—in his book *Electrifying America*:

> *In the beginning Americans believed that electricity would free them from toil, as prophesied in the popular press. . . . Extravagant predictions about the electrified future were an integral part of the new technology's social meaning. Americans learned that they might use electricity to abolish sleep, cure disease, lose weight, quicken intelligence, eliminate pollution, banish housework, and much more. But few of the predictions of amateurs and "experts," from Edison to the technocrats, were realized, as the actual development of electrical technologies seldom lived up to expectations.*[3]

Although information technology is a far less revolutionary technology than electricity, it has nevertheless spurred a particularly extreme version of this phenomenon, which culminated in the millennial fervor of the 1990s, when visions of digital utopias became commonplace. With an almost religious zeal, the metaphysicians of the Internet promised to free us from the burdens and constraints of our physical selves and release us into a new and purified world of cyberspace. The sense of an impending revolution quickly spread to the business realm, as the notion of virtual commerce took hold of executives' and investors' imaginations. The authors of *Unleashing the Killer App* captured the zeitgeist well in 1998 when they described the Internet as a "primordial soup" from which an entirely new business world was emerging. Making the transition to this new world wouldn't be so hard, they assured us: "Since corporations are themselves imaginary creatures, doing business in a virtual location requires relatively little in the way of adaptation."[4]

Such extravagant claims have become rarer since the Internet boom went bust. But even today, the desire to see IT as a revolutionary force that "changes everything" remains strong. A columnist for the *Toronto Globe and Mail* tells us that while the importance of the Internet may be ebbing, "another wave, which I call the Hypernet, is just rolling in."[5] *Business-Week* proclaims the emergence of "a global digital nervous system whose potential impact seems almost limitless."[6] A group of IT consultants claim that a new and magical kind of software for "business process management" will enable executives to reshape their organizations with a few clicks of a mouse.[7] Untangling the real from the fantastic remains a difficult challenge.

It would therefore seem appropriate to end this book by stepping back and gauging in broad terms the real impact of IT, not just on business but on society in general. Unfortunately, that's much easier said than done. Although we're now five decades into the so-called computer revolution, it remains difficult to judge with any precision the extent and shape of IT's effects. Has it been truly transformative? Will it become truly transformative? The fact is, we can't yet answer those questions with any certainty. The best we can do is to separate what we do know from what we don't, and to look ahead with a mix of curiosity, skepticism, and humility.

Certainly, IT's ubiquity is striking. Computers are everywhere, and they seem to be doing almost everything. They have simplified computations of all sorts and have given us easy access to enormous stores of information. Connected through the Internet, they have changed the way we communicate, gather information, and, in some cases, shop and carry out other everyday transactions. Applying their enormous computational power, companies have automated myriad tasks that used to be done manually, speeding up many activities and often reducing costs substantially. But has IT *fundamentally* changed the way we live or work? It's hard to make the case that it has. If you plucked someone out of, say, the 1930s and set him loose in the world today, would he be able to make sense of what he sees? The answer is yes. The basic structures, institutions, and routines of society and commerce, including business organizations and processes, have not changed as much as we might like to think. We're still very much the children of the Second Industrial Revolution.

Indeed, compared to the cataclysmic changes in society and business brought about by the new technologies of the late nineteenth century—not just rail, telegraph, telephone, and electricity but also the internal combustion engine, refrigeration, air-conditioning, photography, and indoor plumbing—the changes wrought by the new technologies of the late twentieth century seem modest, an extension of the past rather than a break with it. Life is unthinkable without the advances of the nineteenth century. The same can't be said of information technology. Ask yourself which you'd rather do without: Your computer or your toilet? Your Internet connection or your light bulbs?[8]

Even IT's role in improving productivity remains the subject of debate. Through the first four decades of the great IT buildout, U.S. productivity growth didn't budge from its sluggish pace, leading economist Robert Solow to his famous 1987 observation: "[Y]ou can see the computer age everywhere but in the productivity statistics."[9] The sudden surge in productivity during the late 1990s seemed to solve Solow's "productivity paradox," to make obvious at last IT's power to boost industrial output without requiring an offsetting increase in input. New academic studies were published that convincingly documented the link between computerization and productivity. A February 2000 report by two economists at the Federal Reserve Board, for example, argued that while the use of computers "made a relatively small contribution" to productivity growth through the early 1990s, "this contribution surged in the second half of the decade." The researchers concluded that "information technology has been the key factor behind the improved productivity."[10]

In a speech on March 6, 2000, the usually cautious Federal Reserve chairman Alan Greenspan explicitly attributed "the resurgence in productivity growth" to "the revolution in information technology." He then went on to state what at the time seemed obvious:

At the end of the day, the benefits of new technologies can be realized only if they are embodied in capital investment, defined to include any outlay that increases the value of the firm. For these investments to be made, the prospective rate of return must exceed the cost of capital. Technological synergies have enlarged the set of productive capital investments, while lofty equity values and declining prices of high-tech equipment have reduced the cost of capital. The result has been a veritable explosion of spending on high-tech equipment and software, which has raised the growth of the capital stock dramatically over the past five years. The fact that the capital spending boom is still going strong indicates that businesses continue to find a wide array of potential high-rate-of-return, productivity-enhancing investments. And I see nothing to suggest that these opportunities will peter out any time soon.[11]

As it turned out, of course, Greenspan's ebullient comments marked the peak of both the bull market and the IT spending boom. As we have since come to realize, moreover, many of the seemingly "high-rate-of-return" IT investments in the 1990s ended up producing no return whatsoever for the companies that made them—much of what was purchased is not even being used. That doesn't mean that, at a broad level, the massive expansion of IT capital stock won't ultimately pay off for the economy as a whole, leading to higher overall productivity and better living standards. Indeed, the strong continued expansion in U.S. productivity since the turn of the century seems to be, in large part, a product of the IT investments of the 1990s, which have enabled companies to do more with fewer employees.[12]

Still, there remains a good deal of uncertainty about the nature and strength of the link between IT and productivity. Why, it's often asked, have some countries and industries that invested heavily in IT enjoyed robust productivity growth while other big investors have not? The discrepancies in the productivity surge of the 1990s have been well documented by the McKinsey Global Institute. Its study of productivity growth during the decade found that the great majority of the gain was concentrated in just a few industries, particularly those involved in producing computers and related products. McKinsey found that three IT-related sectors—semiconductors, computer assembly, and telecommunications—contributed 36 percent of the productivity growth from 1993 through 2000, even though they represented just 8 percent of the U.S. economy. Three other industries—retailing, wholesaling, and securities brokerage—contributed an additional 40 percent of the productivity growth, though they represented only 24 percent of the economy. In total, therefore, six industries representing 32 percent of gross domestic product accounted for 76 percent of the productivity growth. All other industries saw either slight gains or actual declines.

Within the six sectors showing particularly rapid productivity growth, moreover, IT was "one of many operational factors contributing to the jump," according to McKinsey. Although the innovative use of IT was certainly very important, the "crucial catalyst" was, simply, "heightened competitive intensity," which forced managers to pursue all sorts of creative ways to increase their companies' efficiency.[13] Perhaps most striking of all, McKinsey found only one industry in which the Internet generated a material increase in productivity. And what was that industry? Ironically, it was securities brokerage, which gained a significant boost from on-line stock trading—the very innovation that has come to stand as a symbol of the excesses of the era.[14]

In their extensive studies of IT's role in productivity growth, Erik Brynjolfsson and Lorin Hitt also stress the importance of "complementary investments." It usually takes many years, they show, for IT to lift a company's productivity substantially, and the gains hinge as much on related process and organizational innovations as on the original technology itself. Indeed, they write, the "complementary investments in 'organizational capital' . . . may be up to ten times as large as the direct investments in computers."[15] The emerging consensus among economists seems to be that in some industries IT can boost productivity considerably, even dramatically, but only when it's combined with broader changes in business practice, competition, and regulatory control. In isolation, it tends to be inert.

Determining IT's influence on productivity is critical. It will help economists and politicians make more accurate forecasts of future economic conditions, and it will help guide government decisions about how and where to invest in and otherwise promote the expansion of their countries' and regions' IT infrastructures. But beyond the question of IT's effect on productivity lie other important issues, many of which have not received enough attention.

As was the case with earlier infrastructural technologies, heavy investments in IT have led to what economists call "capital deepening" within companies—the replacement of labor with equipment. Simply put, computers have taken on the work that used to be done by people. When economic growth is strong—when output rises faster than productivity—that kind of trade-off pays off not just for individual companies but for the whole economy and hence the whole society. The commercial sector becomes steadily more efficient, displaced workers rapidly move into new jobs, and general living standards rise.

But if productivity growth races ahead of economic growth, a very different and altogether less attractive economic dynamic may play out. The stock of jobs may begin to decline, unemployment may drift upward, the supply of goods may outstrip demand, prices may drop, and the divide between the wealthy and the poor may grow wider and deeper. We have, it's worth noting, seen signs of all these phenomena in the recent history of the U.S. economy. It would be rash to jump to the conclusion that strong productivity gains from IT investment will end up doing harm as well as good—the resiliency of the American economy is hard to overstate—but it would also be rash to dismiss the possibility out of hand.

If, in fact, we look back to the second half of the nineteenth century, we find a troubling precedent. In the 1870s, the world was also emerging from a technology-inspired spending spree. The rapid expansion of rail, shipping, and telegraph lines opened the door to global free trade and inspired massive capital investment. The resulting combination of rapidly increasing production, surging productivity, fierce competition, and widespread industrial overcapacity set the stage for nearly three solid decades of deflation, despite the continued expansion of the world economy. In Britain, the dominant economic power of the time, the overall level of prices dropped a staggering 40 percent.[16] In the United States, prices for most products decreased steadily from 1867 through 1897.

The prophecy of the *Mechanics Magazine* writer—"greater will be the cheapness of everything"—came to pass, though with different and more complex effects than he had imagined. Profits fell along with prices, and businesses suffered. As economic malaise spread, the belief in unbridled commercial opportunity that had taken hold in the middle years of the century died away. Workers lost their jobs, farmers and laborers rebelled, and countries began to rebuild barriers to trade. As the historian D.S. Landes put it, "Optimism about a future of indefinite progress gave way to uncertainty and a sense of agony." [17]

The world is much different today, of course. We understand the dynamics of a global economy better than our nineteenth-century forebears did, and we have better mechanisms in place to monitor commerce and trade. History is unlikely to repeat itself. Nevertheless, it's important to remember that the introduction of a new infrastructural technology can have complex and often unpredictable consequences. We should not be complacent about the intensification of deflationary pressures, the shift of skilled technical jobs to low-labor-cost countries, and the erosion of traditional competitive advantages. While information technology isn't changing everything, it is changing many things. Some of the changes are for the better and some for the worse, but all demand close and clear-eyed attention.

Notes

Preface

1. Throughout this book, I use the terms "information technology" and "IT," as they are the terms most widely used in the United States. In other areas of the world, the somewhat more precise terms "information and communications technology" and "ICT" have come into favor. As commonly used, I believe "IT" and "ICT" are interchangeable in meaning, and I use "IT" with that understanding.

2. In fact, the center of innovation for the IT industry appears to be shifting from the business to the consumer market. With home PCs increasingly being used for video editing, audio and image processing, and graphics-intensive gaming, the average home computer user today has a greater need for additional processing power and innovative new software than the average business user.

Chapter 1

1. Rob Walker, "Interview with Marcian (Ted) Hoff," *Silicon Genesis: Oral Histories of Semiconductor Industry Pioneers,* 3 March 1995, <http://www.stanford.edu/group/mmdd/SiliconValley/SiliconGenesis/TedHoff/Hoff.html> (accessed 16 June 2003). See also Jeffrey Zygmont, *Microchip: An Idea, Its Genesis, and the Revolution It Created* (Cambridge, MA: Perseus, 2003), 104–119.

2. U.S. Department of Commerce, *The Emerging Digital Economy,* April 1998, 6.

3. Gartner Dataquest, "Update: IT Spending," June 2003, <http://www.dataquest.com/press_gartner/quickstats/ITSpending.html> (accessed 13 August 2003).

4. "The Compass World IT Strategy Census 1998–2000," (Rotterdam, The Netherlands: Compass Publishing BV, 1998) 4–5.

5. Jack Welch with John A. Byrne, *Jack: Straight from the Gut* (New York: Warner Books, 2001), 341–351.

6. Adrian Slywotzky and Richard Wise, "An Unfinished Revolution," *MIT Sloan Management Review* 44, no. 3 (Spring 2003): 94.

7. Blackstone Technology Group, "Blackstone Technology Group—Expertise," <http://www.bstonetech.com/Expertise_4.asp > (accessed 28 June 2003).

8. Brad Boston, "Cisco Systems' CIO Brad Boston Responds to Nicholas G. Carr's Article 'IT Doesn't Matter,'" 25 June 2003, <http://newsroom.cisco.com/dlls/hd_062503.html> (accessed 26 June 2003).

9. Microsoft, "What .NET Means for IT Professionals," 24 July 2002, <http://www.microsoft.com/net/business/it_pros.asp> (accessed 28 June 2003).

Chapter 2

1. "Competition of Locomotive Carriages on the Liverpool and Manchester Railway," *Mechanics Magazine,* 17 October 1829, as transcribed at Resco Railways Web site <http://www.resco.co.uk/rainhill/rain2.html> (accessed 8 February 2003). The impact of the railroads would be even greater in the United States, as Alfred Chandler has noted, due to the country's greater geographic expanse and less developed industrial base. See Alfred D. Chandler Jr., *Scale and Scope: The Dynamics of Industrial Capitalism* (Cambridge: Harvard University Press, 1990), 252.

2. See, for example, Edward Chancellor, *Devil Take the Hindmost: A History of Financial Speculation* (New York: Farrar, Straus and Giroux, 1999), 150–151.

3. Chandler, *Scale and Scope,* 65.

4. Tom Standage, *The Victorian Internet* (New York: Walker & Company, 1998), 167–168.

5. Sam H. Schurr et al., *Electricity in the American Economy: Agent of Technological Progress* (Westport, CT: Greenwood Press, 1990), 27.

6. See David E. Nye, *Electrifying America: Social Meanings of a New Technology* (Cambridge: MIT Press, 1990), 185–237.

7. Schurr et al., *Electricity in the American Economy,* 21–26.

8. See Amy Friedlander, *Power and Light: Electricity in the U.S. Energy Infrastructure, 1870–1940* (Reston, VA: CNRI, 1996), 62–63.

9. As quoted in Schurr et al., *Electricity in the American Economy,* 32. See also Richard B. DuBoff, *Electric Power in American Manufacturing, 1889–1958* (New York: Arno Press, 1979), 139–148.

10. Friedlander, *Power and Light,* 62.

11. Chandler, *Scale and Scope,* 58–59.

12. See Alfred D. Chandler Jr., *The Visible Hand* (Cambridge: Harvard University Press, 1977), 249–253.

13. For more on Hershey, see Joel Glenn Brenner, *The Emperors of Chocolate: Inside the Secret World of Hershey and Mars* (New York: Random House, 1999).

14. Eric Hobsbawm, *The Age of Capital: 1848–1875* (New York: Vintage, 1996), 310.

15. Ibid., 59.

16. Standage, *The Victorian Internet,* 58.

17. DuBoff, *Electric Power in American Manufacturing, 1889–1958,* 43.

18. John Brooks, *Telephone: The First Hundred Years* (New York: Harper & Row, 1976), 69, 108, 187.

19. Tomas Nonnenmacher, "History of the U.S. Telegraph Industry," *EH.Net Encyclopedia of Economic and Business History,* 15 August 2001, <http://www.eh.net/encyclopedia/nonnenmacher.industry.tele graphic.us.php> (accessed 20 June 2003).

20. Nye, *Electrifying America,* 261.

21. See, for example, Bryan Glick, "IT Suppliers Racing to Be an Indispensable Utility," *Computing,* 16 April 2003, <http://www. computingnet.co.uk/Computingopinion/1140261> (accessed 18 June 2003).

Chapter 3

1. In this chapter and this book, I use the terms "commodity" and "commoditization" from the user's perspective. A resource becomes a commodity, in this view, when it is readily available to all competitors and therefore provides no lasting distinction to any one company. A commodity input for a user is not necessarily a commodity product for a supplier. Think of Microsoft Office. No company gains an edge by buying a license to use Office—it's a commodity input shared by most companies. For Microsoft, however, Office is anything but a commodity. Through various means—control of the PC desktop, manipulation of standards and compatibility, network effects, and high user switching costs—Microsoft has been able to continue to sell Office at a premium price and earn enormous profits from what is now a mundane product.

2. Kathryn Jones, "The Dell Way," *Business 2.0*, February 2003, 60.

3. Andrew Park and Peter Burrows, "Dell, the Conqueror," *BusinessWeek,* 24 September 2001, 92.

4. Ibid.

5. "Modifying Moore's Law," *The Economist,* Survey: The IT Industry, 10 May 2003, 5.

6. John Markoff and Steve Lohr, "Intel's Huge Bet Turns Iffy," *New York Times,* 29 September 2002.

7. Aaron Ricadela, "Amazon Says It's Spending Less on IT," *Information Week,* 31 October 2001, <http://www.informationweek.com/story/IWK20011031S0005> (accessed 7 July 2003).

8. Richard Waters, "In Search of More for Less," *Financial Times,* 29 April 2003.

9. See Daniel Roth, "Can EMC Restore Its Glory?" *Fortune,* 8 July 2002, 107.

10. Jones, "The Dell Way."

11. Clayton M. Christensen, *The Innovator's Dilemma: When New Technologies Cause Great Firms to Fail* (Boston: Harvard Business School Press, 1997), xxii. See also chapter 8 of Christensen's book.

12. See "Moving Up the Stack," *The Economist,* Survey: The IT Industry, 10 May 2003, 6.

13. Steve Lohr, *Go To* (New York: Basic Books, 2001), 8. Lohr makes an accurate point about software in general. The problem arises when people confuse innovation potential with practical value, assuming that the lack of limits on software development necessarily implies a lack of limits to its usefulness in business. This view is widespread in IT circles and was often reflected in critical responses to my *Harvard Business Review* article "IT Doesn't Matter." An *Industry Week* columnist, for example, wrote, "Software can best be likened to that from which it is spawned: brainpower. The limits to the nature, applications and functions of software lie in the human brain. The different applications of business software are almost innumerable." (Doug Bartholomew, "Yes, Nicholas, IT *Does* Matter," *Industry Week,* 1 September 2003, <http://www.industryweek.com/Columns/Asp/columns.asp?ColumnId=955> [accessed 5 October 2003].) A prominent IT consultant similarly argued that "software, developed and run on commodity hardware, represents a virtually unlimited source of profitable innovation." (Peter O'Farrell, "Carr Goes Off the Rail," Cutter Consortium Executive Update 4, no. 7, 2003, <http://www.cutter.com/freestuff/bttu0307.html#ofarrell> [accessed 4 October 2003].) The use of the adjective "profitable" turns this from a statement of fact to one of speculation.

14. Martin Campbell-Kelly, *From Airline Reservations to Sonic the Hedgehog: A History of the Software Industry* (Cambridge: MIT Press, 2003), 31–34.

15. Ibid., 71.

16. See, for example, Philip J. Gill, "ERP: Keep it Simple," *Information Week,* 9 August 1999, <http://www.informationweek.com/747/47aderp.htm> (accessed 12 July 2003).

17. John Foley, "Oracle Targets ERP Integration," *Information Week,* 30 March 1998, <http://www.informationweek.com/675/75iuora.htm> (accessed 8 July 2003).

18. Campbell-Kelly, *History of the Software Industry,* 195.

19. See Sam H. Schurr et al., *Electricity in the American Economy:*

Agent of Technological Progress (Westport, CT: Greenwood Press, 1990), 43–49.

20. Carl Shapiro and Hal R. Varian, *Information Rules: A Strategic Guide to the Network Economy* (Boston: Harvard Business School Press, 1999), 193–194.

21. Netcraft, "July 2003 Web Server Survey," <http://news.netcraft.com/archives/2003/07/02/july_2003_web_server_survey.html> (accessed 7 July 2003).

22. Lohr, *Go To*, 6–7.

23. Richard Waters, "In Search of More for Less," *Financial Times,* 29 April 2003; Paul Taylor, "GE: Trailblazing the Indian Phenomenon," *Financial Times,* 2 July 2003.

24. Nuala Moran, "Looking for Savings on Distant Horizons," *Financial Times,* 2 July 2003.

25. Ibid.

26. Kumar Mahadeva, conversation with author, 16 June 2003.

27. John Seely Brown and John Hagel III, letter to the editor, *Harvard Business Review,* July 2003, 111.

28. Scott Thurm and Nick Wingfield, "How Titans Swallowed Wi-Fi, Stifling Silicon Valley Uprising," *Wall Street Journal,* 8 August 2003.

29. Because the emergence of a service-oriented architecture could fundamentally change the way companies buy and use information technology, the stakes for vendors are very high. To date, the conflicting interests of vendors have undermined attempts to arrive at a single set of open standards for Web services, which is crucial to the creation of the architecture. As this book went to press, the prospects for an agreement on standards appeared increasingly dim, at least in the short run. As *CIO* magazine reported in late 2003, noting the appearance of competing standards bodies, "The Web services standards process began to fall apart this year." Christopher Koch, "The Battle for Web Services," *CIO,* 1 October 2003, <http://www.cio.com/archive/100103/standards.html> (accessed 25 November 2003).

30. For a more optimistic view of the potential strategic implications of Web services, see John Seely Brown and John Hagel III, "Flexible IT, Better Strategy," *McKinsey Quarterly* no. 4 (2003),

<http://www.mckinseyquarterly.com/article_page.asp?ar=1346&L2
=13&L3=12&srid=14&gp=1> (accessed 10 October 2003).

31. Given the endless creativity of software writers, it's not hard to imagine the development of a Web service that enables companies to monitor how their competitors are using other Web services at any given moment. The capability for rapid replication would thus be built right into the architecture.

32. Scott McNealy, keynote speech at SunNetwork 2003 conference, San Francisco, 16 September 2003, <www.sun.com/about sun/media/presskits/networkcomputing03q3/mcnealykeynote.pdf> (accessed 1 October 2003).

33. Mylene Mangalindan, "Oracle's Larry Ellison Expects Greater Innovation from Sector," *Wall Street Journal,* 8 April 2003.

34. Robert J. Gordon, "Does the New Economy Measure Up to the Great Inventions of the Past?" *Journal of Economic Perspectives* 4, no. 14 (Fall 2000): 62. See also Robert J. Gordon, "Hi-Tech Innovation and Productivity Growth: Does Supply Create Its Own Demand?" NBER working paper, 19 December 2002.

35. Tony Comper, "Back to the Future: A CEO's Perspective on the IT Post-Revolution," speech at the IBM Global Financial Services Forum, San Francisco, 8 September 2003, <http://www2.bmo. com/speech/article/0,1259,contentCode-3294_divId-4_langId-1_nav Code-124,00.html> (accessed 23 September 2003).

36. Not everyone in the IT industry assumes a future of unlimited growth. Oracle CIO Larry Ellison incurred the wrath of many of his colleagues when in an early 2003 *Wall Street Journal* article he questioned "this bizarre notion . . . that we'll never be a mature industry" and suggested that the IT business might already be "as large as it's going to be." (Mylene Mangalindan, "Oracle's Larry Ellison Expects Greater Innovation from Sector," *Wall Street Journal,* 8 April 2003.) At the 2003 World Economic Forum in Davos, Switzerland, Bill Joy, the cofounder of Sun Microsystems, posed a discomforting question: "What if the reality is that people have already bought most of the stuff they want to own?" (Mark Landler, "Titans Still Gather at Davos, Shorn of Profits and Bavado," *New York Times,* 27 January 2003.) Even Hewlett-Packard CEO Carly Fiorina openly predicts a

dramatic shakeout in the IT industry as companies adapt to a significant slowing in its rate of growth. (See Quentin Hardy, "We Did It," *Forbes*, 11 August 2003, 76.)

Chapter 4

1. Lorin M. Hitt and Erik Brynjolfsson, "Productivity, Business Profitability, and Consumer Surplus: Three *Different* Measures of Information Technology Value," *MIS Quarterly* 20, no. 2 (June 1996): 121–142.

2. Erik Brynjolfsson and Lorin Hitt, "Paradox Lost? Firm-Level Evidence on the Returns to Information Systems Spending," *Management Science* 42, no. 4 (April 1996): 541–558.

3. Hitt and Brynjolfsson, "Productivity, Business Profitability, and Consumer Surplus," 131.

4. Ibid., 134-135.

5. Ibid., 139.

6. Baba Prasad and Patrick T. Harker, "Examining the Contribution of Information Technology Toward Productivity and Profitability in U.S. Retail Banking," Wharton Financial Institutions Center Working Paper 97-09, March 1997, 18.

7. Brynjolfsson, it's important to note, believes that IT innovation continues to offer individual firms the potential for competitive advantage, although he points out that any advantage would tend to come not from the technology itself but from organizational, people, and process changes made in the wake of installing the technology. See Erik Brynjolfsson, "The IT Productivity Gap," *Optimize,* July 2003 <http://www.optimizemag.com/printer/021/pr_roi.html> (accessed 8 September 2003).

8. J. Bradford Delong, "Macroeconomic Implications of the 'New Economy,'" May 2000, <http://www.j-bradford-delong.net/OpEd/virtual/ne_macro.html> (accessed 13 January 2003).

9. Martin Campbell-Kelly, *From Airline Reservations to Sonic the Hedgehog: A History of the Software Industry* (Cambridge: MIT Press, 2003), 14–15.

10. Robert H'obbes' Zakon, "Hobbes' Internet Timeline v. 6.1," 2003, <http://www.zakon.org/robert/internet/timeline> (accessed 23 January 2003).

11. Olga Kharif "The Fiber-Optic 'Glut'—in a New Light," *BusinessWeek Online,* 31 August 2001, <http://www.businessweek.com/bwdaily/dnflash/aug2001/nf20010831_396.htm> (accessed 18 December 2002>.

12. Brian Hayes, "The First Fifty Years," *CIO Insight,* 1 November 2001, <http://www.cioinsight.com/article2/0,3959,49331,00.asp> (accessed 12 June 2003).

13. Campbell-Kelly, *A History of the Software Industry,* 30.

14. Martin Campbell-Kelly and William Aspray, *Computer: A History of the Information Machine* (New York: BasicBooks, 1996), 169.

15. Leslie Goff, "Sabre Takes Off," *Computerworld,* 22 March 1999, <http://www.computerworld.com/news/1999/story/0,11280,34992,00.html> (accessed 27 June 2003).

16. Campbell-Kelly, *A History of the Software Industry,* 45.

17. Thomas Petzinger Jr., *Hard Landing: The Epic Contest for Power and Profits That Plunged the Airlines into Chaos* (New York: Times Books, 1995), 55.

18. See "American Hospital Supply Corporation: The ASAP System (A)," Harvard Business School Case # 9-186-005, 1988.

19. Ibid., 1.

20. Charles Marshall, Benn Konsynski, and John Sviokla, "Baxter International: OnCall as Soon as Possible?" Harvard Business School Case #9-195-103, 1994 (revised 29 March 1996), 7.

21. For more on Reuters, see Donald Read, *The Power of News: The History of Reuters, 1849–1989* (Oxford: Oxford University Press, 1992).

22. Progressive Policy Institute, "Computer Costs Are Plummeting," *The New Economy Index,* November 1998, <http://www.neweconomyindex.org/section1_page12.html> (accessed 12 January 2003).

23. Steve Lohr, *Go To* (New York: Basic Books, 2001), 162.

24. Erik Brynjolfsson and Lorin M. Hitt, "Beyond Computation: Information Technology, Organizational Transformation and Business Performance," *Journal of Economic Perspectives* 14. no. 4 (2000): 26.

25. Security concerns can also deter a company from using the Internet to carry out sensitive transactions.

26. Thomas H. Davenport, "Putting the Enterprise into the Enterprise System," *Harvard Business Review,* July–August 1998, 121–131.

27. See, for example, Philip J. Gill, "ERP: Keep It Simple," *Information Week,* 9 August 1999, <http://www.informationweek.com/747/47aderp.htm> (accessed 12 July 2003).

28. Kevin Lynch, "Network Software: Finding the Perfect Fit," *Inbound Logistics,* November 2002, <http://www.inboundlogistics.com/articles/itmatters/itmatters1102.shtml> (accessed 8 July 2003).

29. Erik Brynjolfsson and Lorin M. Hitt, "Computing Productivity: Firm-Level Evidence," MIT Sloan Working Paper 4210-01, June 2003, 26.

30. Carlota Perez, *Technological Revolutions and Financial Capital: The Dynamics of Bubbles and Golden Ages* (Cheltenham: Edward Elgar, 2002), 36.

31. Ibid., 4.

32. Ibid., 134-135.

Chapter 5

1. Michael E. Porter, *Competitive Advantage: Creating and Sustaining Superior Performance* (New York: Free Press, 1985), 164.

2. Mark Cotteleer, "An Empirical Study of Operational Performance Convergence Following Enterprise IT Implementation," Harvard Business School Working Paper 03-011, October 2002.

3. Bill Gates, *The Road Ahead,* 2nd edition (New York: Penguin, 1996), 180–181.

4. Michael E. Porter, "Strategy and the Internet," *Harvard Business Review,* March 2001, 66.

5. Rajen Madan, Carsten Sørenson, and Susan V. Scott, "'Strategy Sort of Died Around April of Last Year for a Lot of Us': CIO Perceptions on ICT Value and Strategy in the UK Financial Sector," paper presented at the 11th European Conference on Information Systems, Naples, Italy, 19–21 June 2003, 10.

6. Quoted in Michael Schrage, "Wal-Mart Trumps Moore's Law," *Technology Review,* March 2002, 21.

7. Joan Magretta, with Nan Stone, *What Management Is: How It Works and Why It's Everyone's Business* (New York: Free Press, 2002), 62. Magretta's book provides an excellent overview of the development of both Dell's and Wal-Mart's strategies, which I have drawn on in my own discussion of these companies.

8. I originally introduced the concept of leverageable advantage in the context of Internet competition in an article in 2000. See Nicholas G. Carr, "Be What You Aren't," *Industry Standard,* 7 August 2000, 162.

9. Due to the current flux of the music industry, it remains to be seen whether Apple will be able to defend its early lead in on-line retailing. Its advantage may prove sustainable, or it may need to be treated as another leverageable advantage. But in any case, the launch of its music store will have paid off through increased sales of the iPod and other hardware.

10. Don Tapscott, "Rethinking Strategy in a Networked World," *Strategy and Business,* Issue 24, Third Quarter 2001, 39.

11. Larry Downes and Chunka Mui, *Unleashing the Killer App: Digital Strategies for Market Dominance* (Boston: Harvard Business School Press, 1998), 42.

12. R.H. Coase, "The Nature of the Firm," *Economica,* November 1937, 392–393.

13. Coase originally called these costs "marketing costs," but "transaction costs" has become the common term.

14. Hal R. Varian, "If There Was a New Economy, Why Wasn't There a New Economics?" *New York Times,* 17 January 2002.

15. Coase, "The Nature of the Firm," 397 (footnote 3).

16. Ibid., 397. For another view of the different ways that changes in communication costs may influence business organizations, see Thomas W. Malone, *The Future of Work: How the New Order of Business Will Shape Your Organization, Your Management Style, and Your Life* (Boston: Harvard Business School Press, 2004).

17. Andrew McAfee, "New Technologies, Old Organizational Forms? Reassessing the Impact of IT on Markets and Hierarchies," Harvard Business School Working Paper 03-078, April 2003.

18. Varian, "If There Was a New Economy, Why Wasn't There a New Economics?"

19. Richard Veryard, *The Component-Based Business: Plug and Play* (London: Springer, 2000), 2.

20. It was this view that lay behind much of the hype about "electronic B2B markets" in 1999 and 2000. There was a sense then, at least among many proponents of "e-business," that supplier relationships could be reduced to the automatic exchange of data over the Internet. As it turned out, those relationships were more complex, more *human,* than technologists assumed. Today, some of the promoters of Web services and business process management (BPM) echo the arguments of the earlier B2B fad.

21. See Diana Farrell, Terra Terwilliger, and Allen P. Webb, "Getting IT Spending Right this Time," *McKinsey Quarterly,* no. 2 (2003): <http://www.mckinseyquarterly.com/article_page.asp?ar=1285&L2 =13&L3=13> (accessed 14 July 2003).

Chapter 6

1. See Bernard L. Weinstein and Terry L. Clower, "The Impacts of the Union Pacific Service Disruptions on the Texas and National Economies: An Unfinished Story," report prepared for the Railroad Commission of Texas by the University of North Texas Center for Economic Development and Research, 9 February 1998.

2. Robert Ristelhueber and Jennifer Baljko Shah, "Energy Crisis Threatens Silicon Valley's Growth," *EBN,* 19 January 2001, <http://www.ebnonline.com/story/OEG20010119S0033> (accessed 11 August 2003).

3. See, for example, John Baschab and Jon Piot, *The Executive's Guide to Information Technology* (Hoboken, NJ: John Wiley, 2003), 9–11.

4. Standish Group, "The Chaos Report (1994)," Report of the Standish Group, 1994.

5. Standish Group, "Chaos: A Recipe for Success," Report of the Standish Group, 1999.

6. KPMG, "Project Risk Management: Information Risk Management" (London: KPMG U.K., June 1999).

7. Richard Waters, "Corporate Computing Tries to Find a New Path," *Financial Times,* 4 June 2003.

8. James L. McKenney, with Duncan C. Copeland and Richard O. Mason, *Waves of Change: Business Evolution Through Information Technology* (Boston: Harvard Business School Press, 1995), 23.

9. Richard Waters, "Corporate Computing Tries to Find a New Path."

10. Ibid.

11. Carol Hildebrand, "Why Squirrels Manage Storage Better than You Do," *Darwin*, April 2003, <http://www.darwinmag.com/read/040102/squirrels.html> (accessed 10 January 2003).

12. Barbara DePompa Reimers, "Five Cost-Cutting Strategies for Data Storage," *Computerworld*, 21 October 2002, <http://www.computerworld.com/hardwaretopics/storage/story/0,10801,75221,00.html> (accessed 5 February 2003).

13. See Christopher Koch, "Your Open Source Plan," *CIO*, 15 March 2003, 58.

14. Richard Waters, "In Search of More for Less," *Financial Times*, 29 April 2003.

15. Robin Gareiss, "Chief of the Year: Ralph Szygenda," *Information Week*, 2 December 2002, <http://www.informationweek.com/story/IWK20021127S0011> (accessed 23 July 2003).

16. William M. Bulkeley, "CIOs Boost Their Profile as They Become Cost Cutters," *Wall Street Journal*, 11 March 2003.

17. Koch, "Your Open Source Plan," 58–59.

18. Matt Berger, "LinuxWorld: Amazon.com Clicks with Linux," *Computerworld*, 14 August 2002, <http://www.computerworld.com/managementtopics/roi/story/0,10801,73617,00.html> (accessed 22 July 2003).

19. Fiona Harvey, "Michael Dell of Dell Computer," *Financial Times*, 5 August 2003.

20. John Chambers, "The 2nd Industrial Revolution: Why the Internet Changes Everything," keynote address at Oracle AppsWorld 2001, New Orleans, 20–23 February 2001, <http://www.it-global-forum.org/panamit/dscgi/ds.py/Get/File-1056/Page_45-58_Oracle_Bus_Report.pdf> (accessed 15 July 2003).

21. Grady Means, "Economics' New Dimensions: Why They're Extreme, Dramatic and Radical," keynote address at Oracle AppsWorld

2001, New Orleans, 20-23 February 2001, <http://www.it-global forum.org/panamit/dscgi/ds.py/Get/File-1056/Page_45-58_Oracle_ Bus_Report.pdf> (accessed 15 July 2003).

22. See Charles Haddad, "UPS vs. FedEx: Ground Wars," *Business Week,* 21 May 2001, 64.

23. Alinean, "Spending Trends of Best and Worst Performing Companies," correspondence with author, March 2003. Alinean also performed a similar analysis of 1,500 European companies. Here, too, it found that the best-performing companies spent considerably less on IT as a percentage of revenue (2.1 percent) than the average (7.3 percent). See Alinean, "North American Companies Outshine European Peers in IT Spending Efficiency," Alinean press release, 4 March 2003. It's worth noting that the measures that come out of studies like these are averages and shouldn't be considered benchmarks. Different companies will have different spending requirements, depending on their industry, their competitive situation, their past expenditures, and so forth.

24. Tom Pohlmann with Christopher Mines and Meredith Child, *Linking IT Spend to Business Results,* Forrester Research report, October 2002.

25. McKinsey Global Institute, "Whatever Happened to the New Economy?" report of the McKinsey Global Institute, November 2002.

26. Rod Newing and Paul Strassman, "Watch the Economics and the Risk, Not the Technology," *Financial Times,* 5 December 2001.

27. Tim Phillips, "The Bulletin Interview: Larry Ellison," *The Computer Bulletin,* July 2002, <http://www.bcs.org.uk/publicat/ebull/july02/intervie.htm> (accessed 7 January 2003).

28. Jonathan Collins, "The Cost of Wal-Mart's RFID Edict," *RFID Journal,* 10 September 2003, <http://www.rfidjournal.com/article/view/572/1/1/> (accessed 1 October 2003).

29. Carol Sliwa, "Wal-Mart Suppliers Shoulder Burden of Daunting RFID Effort," *Computerworld,* 10 November 2003, <http://www. computerworld.com/news/2003/story/0,11280,86978,00.html> (accessed 25 November 2003).

30. On a related note, the McKinsey Global Institute's research shows that companies tend to gain the greatest productivity increases from applications of IT that are specialized to their particular industry segment. Technologies adopted across industries, such as ERP systems, have much less impact on performance. McKinsey Global Institute, "Whatever Happened to the New Economy?" 29.

31. See Robert D. Austin and Christopher A. R. Darby, "The Myth of Secure Computing," *Harvard Business Review,* June 2003, 120–121.

32. Max D. Hopper, "Rattling SABRE—New Ways to Compete on Information," *Harvard Business Review,* May–June 1990, 125.

Chapter 7

1. Caminer et al., *LEO: The Incredible Story of the World's First Business Computer* (New York: McGraw-Hill, 1998), 228.

2. Ibid., 363.

3. David E. Nye, *Electrifying America: Social Meanings of a New Technology* (Cambridge: MIT Press, 1990), 386.

4. Larry Downes and Chunka Mui, *Unleashing the Killer App: Digital Strategies for Market Dominance* (Boston: Harvard Business School Press, 1998), 31.

5. David Ticoll, "In Writing Off IT, You Write Off Innovation," *Toronto Globe and Mail,* 29 May 2003.

6. Robert D. Hof, "The Quest for the Next Big Thing," *BusinessWeek,* 18–25 August 2003, 92.

7. Howard Smith and Peter Fingar, two of the more ardent proponents of business process management (BPM) software, explained the concept in a 2003 paper entitled "21st Century Business Architecture": "By representing business processes in a mathematically formalized way, processes developed in one part of the business, or by a business partner, can be connected, combined and analyzed in real time, providing a foundation for the true real-time enterprise behind the real-time enterprise slogan. . . . When the business process engineer pushes the 'make it so button,' the computer-aided deployment

part of the system actually implements the mission-critical, end-to-end process across the disparate legacy systems inside the enterprise and across the value chain." <http://www.bpmi.org/bpmi-library/D7B509F211.BPM21CArch.pdf> (accessed 29 September 2003).

8. These questions echo ones posed by Robert J. Gordon in a 2000 article: "Will the information revolution spawned by the computer create as great a change in living conditions as the major inventions of the late nineteenth and early twentieth century? At an intuitive level, it seems unlikely. For instance, we might gather together a group of Houston residents and ask: 'If you could choose only one of the following two inventions, air conditioning or the Internet, which would you choose?' Or we might ask a group of Minneapolis residents, 'If you could choose only one of the following two inventions, indoor plumbing or the Internet, which would you choose?'" See Gordon, "Does the New Economy Measure Up to the Great Inventions of the Past?" *Journal of Economic Perspectives* 4, no. 14 (Fall 2000): 60.

9. Robert M. Solow, "We'd Better Watch Out," *New York Times Book Review,* 12 July 1987, 36.

10. Stephen D. Oliner and Daniel E. Sichel, "The Resurgence of Growth in the Late 1990s: Is Information Technology the Story?" Federal Reserve Board white paper, February 2000, 27. (Later published in *Journal of Economic Perspectives* 14, Fall 2000, 3–22.)

11. Alan Greenspan, "The Revolution in Information Technology," remarks before the Boston College Conference on the New Economy, 6 March 2000, <http://www.federalreserve.gov/BOARD DOCS/SPEECHES/2000/20000306.htm> (accessed 5 August 2003).

12. See, for example, Robert J. Gordon, "Five Puzzles in the Behavior of Productivity, Investment, and Innovation," draft of chapter for World Economic Forum, Global Competitiveness Report, 2003–2004, 10 September 2003, <http://faculty-web.at.northwestern.edu/economics/gordon/WEFTEXT.pdf> (accessed 13 October 2003).

13. McKinsey Global Institute, "Whatever Happened to the New Economy?" (San Francisco: McKinsey & Company, November 2002), 4.

14. William W. Lewis et al., "What's Right with the U.S. Economy," *McKinsey Quarterly,* no. 1 (2002): <http://www.mckinseyquarterly.

com/article_page.asp?L2=19&L3=67&ar=1151&pagenum=1>   (accessed 23 August 2003).

15. Erik Brynjolfsson and Lorin Hitt, "Computing Productivity: Firm-Level Evidence," MIT Sloan Working Paper 4210-01, June 2003, 2.

16. Eric Hobsbawm, *The Age of Empire, 1875–1914* (New York: Vintage, 1989), 37.

17. David S. Landes, *The Unbound Prometheus* (London: Cambridge University Press, 1969), 240–241.

Bibliography

Works Consulted

Alinean. "North American Companies Outshine European Peers in IT Spending Efficiency." Alinean press release, 4 March 2003.

"American Hospital Supply Corporation: The ASAP System (A)." Harvard Business School Case # 9-186-005, 1988.

Austin, Robert D., and Christopher A. R. Darby. "The Myth of Secure Computing." *Harvard Business Review*, June 2003, 120–126.

Bain, David Haward. *Empire Express: Building the First Transcontinental Railroad.* New York: Viking, 1999.

Bartholomew, Doug. "Yes, Nicholas, IT *Does* Matter." *Industry Week,* 1 September 2003. <http://www.industryweek.com/Columns/Asp/columns.asp?ColumnId=955> (accessed 5 October 2003).

Baschab, John, and Jon Piot. *The Executive's Guide to Information Technology.* Hoboken, NJ: John Wiley, 2003.

Berger, Matt. "LinuxWorld: Amazon.com Clicks with Linux." *Computerworld,* 14 August 2002. <http://www.computerworld.com/managementtopics/roi/story/0,10801,73617,00.html> (accessed 22 July 2003).

"Blackstone Technology Group—Expertise." <http://www.bstonetech.com/Expertise_4.asp> (accessed 8 July 2003).

Boston, Brad. "Cisco Systems' CIO Brad Boston Responds to Nicholas G. Carr's Article 'IT Doesn't Matter.'" 25 June 2003.

<http://newsroom.cisco.com/dlls/hd_062503.html> (accessed 26 June 2003).

Brenner, Joel Glenn. *The Emperors of Chocolate: Inside the Secret World of Hershey and Mars.* New York: Random House, 1999.

Brooks, John. *Telephone: The First Hundred Years.* New York: Harper & Row, 1976.

Brown, John Seely, and John Hagel III. "Flexible IT, Better Strategy." *McKinsey Quarterly* no. 4 (2003): <http://www.mckinseyquarterly. com/article_page.asp?ar=1346&L2=13&L3=12&srid=14&gp=1> (accessed 10 October 2003).

———. Letter to the editor. *Harvard Business Review,* July 2003, 111.

Brynjolfsson, Erik. "The IT Productivity Gap." *Optimize,* July 2003. <http://www.optimizemag.com/printer/021/pr_roi.html> (accessed 8 September 2003).

Brynjolfsson, Erik, and Lorin M. Hitt. "Beyond Computation: Information Technology, Organizational Transformation and Business Performance." *Journal of Economic Perspectives* 14. no. 4 (2000): 23–48.

———. "Computing Productivity: Firm-Level Evidence." MIT Sloan Working Paper 4210-01, June 2003.

———. "Paradox Lost? Firm-Level Evidence on the Returns to Information Systems Spending." *Management Science* 42, no. 4 (April 1996): 541–558.

Bulkeley, William M. "CIOs Boost Their Profile as They Become Cost Cutters." *Wall Street Journal,* 11 March 2003.

Caminer, David, John Aris, Peter Hermon, and Frank Land. *LEO: The Incredible Story of the World's First Business Computer.* New York, McGraw-Hill, 1998.

Campbell-Kelly, Martin. *From Airline Reservations to Sonic the Hedgehog: A History of the Software Industry.* Cambridge: MIT Press, 2003.

Campbell-Kelly, Martin, and William Aspray. *Computer: A History of the Information Machine.* New York: BasicBooks, 1996.

Carr, Nicholas G. "Be What You Aren't." *Industry Standard,* 7 August 2000, 162.

———. "The Growing Specter of Deflation." *Boston Globe,* 8 June 2003.

————. "IT Doesn't Matter." *Harvard Business Review,* May 2003, 41–49.

Cassidy, John. *Dot.con: The Greatest Story Ever Sold.* New York: HarperCollins, 2002.

Ceruzzi, Paul E. *A History of Modern Computing.* 2d ed. Cambridge: MIT Press, 2003.

Chambers, John. "The 2nd Industrial Revolution: Why the Internet Changes Everything." Keynote address at Oracle AppsWorld 2001, New Orleans, 20–23 February 2001. <http://www.it-globalforum. org/panamit/dscgi/ds.py/Get/File-1056/Page_45-58_Oracle_ Bus_Report.pdf> (accessed 15 July 2003).

Chancellor, Edward. *Devil Take the Hindmost: A History of Financial Speculation.* New York: Farrar, Straus and Giroux, 1999.

Chandler, Alfred D. Jr. *Scale and Scope: The Dynamics of Industrial Capitalism.* Cambridge: Harvard University Press, 1990.

————. *The Visible Hand.* Cambridge: Harvard University Press, 1977.

Christensen, Clayton M. *The Innovator's Dilemma: When New Technologies Cause Great Firms to Fail.* Boston: Harvard Business School Press, 1997.

Coase, R.H. "The Nature of the Firm." *Economica,* November 1937, 386–405.

Collins, Jonathan "The Cost of Wal-Mart's RFID Edict." RFID Journal, 10 September 2003. <http://www.rfidjournal.com/article/ view/572/1/1/> (accessed 1 October 2003).

"The Compass World IT Strategy Census 1998–2000." Rotterdam, The Netherlands: Compass Publishing BV, 1998.

Comper, Tony. "Back to the Future: A CEO's Perspective on the IT Post-Revolution." Speech at the IBM Global Financial Services Forum, San Francisco, 8 September 2003. <http://www2.bmo. com/speech/article/0,1259,contentCode-3294_divId-4_langId-1_ navCode-124,00.html> (accessed 23 September 2003).

"Competition of Locomotive Carriages on the Liverpool and Manchester Railway." *Mechanics Magazine,* 17 October 1829. As transcribed at Resco Railways Web site. <http://www.resco.co.uk/ rainhill/rain2.html> (accessed 8 February 2003).

Cotteleer, Mark. "An Empirical Study of Operational Performance

Convergence Following Enterprise IT Implementation." Harvard Business School Working Paper 03-011, October 2002.

Davenport, Thomas H. *Mission Critical: Realizing the Promise of Enterprise Systems.* Boston: Harvard Business School Press, 2000.

———. "Putting the Enterprise into the Enterprise System." *Harvard Business Review*, July–August 1998, 121–131.

Delong, J. Bradford. "Macroeconomic Implications of the 'New Economy.'" May 2000. <http://www.j-bradford-delong.net/Op Ed/virtual/ne_macro.html> (accessed 13 January 2003).

Downes, Larry, and Chunka Mui. *Unleashing the Killer App: Digital Strategies for Market Dominance.* Boston: Harvard Business School Press, 1998.

DuBoff, Richard B. *Electric Power in American Manufacturing, 1889–1958.* New York: Arno Press, 1979.

Farrell, Diana, Terra Terwilliger, and Allen P. Webb. "Getting IT Spending Right this Time." *McKinsey Quarterly* no. 2 (2003). <http://www.mckinseyquarterly.com/article_page.asp?ar=1285& L2=13&L3=13> (accessed 14 July 2003).

Foley, John. "Oracle Targets ERP Integration." *Information Week*, 30 March 1998. <http://www.informationweek.com/675/75iuora. htm> (accessed 8 July 2003).

Friedlander, Amy. *Emerging Infrastructure: The Growth of Railroads.* Reston: CNRI, 1995.

———. *Power and Light: Electricity in the U.S. Energy Infrastructure, 1870–1940.* Reston, VA: CNRI, 1996.

Gareiss, Robin. "Chief of the Year: Ralph Szygenda." *Information Week*, 2 December 2002. <http://www.informationweek.com/ story/IWK20021127S0011> (accessed 23 July 2003).

Gartner Dataquest. "Update: IT Spending." June 2003 <http:// www.dataquest.com/press_gartner/quickstats/ITSpending.html> (accessed 13 August 2003).

Gates, Bill. *The Road Ahead.* 2nd ed. New York: Penguin, 1996.

Gill, Philip J. "ERP: Keep It Simple." *Information Week*, 9 August 1999. <http://www.informationweek.com/747/47aderp.htm> (accessed 12 July 2003).

Glick, Bryan. "IT Suppliers Racing to Be an Indispensable Utility."

Computing, 16 April 2003. <http://www.computingnet.co.uk/Computingopinion/1140261> (accessed 18 June 2003).

Goff, Leslie. "Sabre Takes Off." *Computerworld,* 22 March 1999. <http://www.computerworld.com/news/1999/story/0,11280,34 992,00.html> (accessed 27 June 2003).

Gordon, Robert J. "Does the New Economy Measure Up to the Great Inventions of the Past?" *Journal of Economic Perspectives* 4, no. 14 (Fall 2000): 49–74.

————. "Five Puzzles in the Behavior of Productivity, Investment, and Innovation." Draft of chapter for World Economic Forum, Global Competitiveness Report, 2003–2004, 10 September 2003. <http://faculty-web.at.northwestern.edu/economics/gordon/ WEFTEXT.pdf> (accessed 13 October 2003).

————. "Hi-Tech Innovation and Productivity Growth: Does Supply Create Its Own Demand?" NBER working paper, 19 December 2002.

Greenspan, Alan. "The Revolution in Information Technology." Remarks before the Boston College Conference on the New Economy, 6 March 2000. <http://www.federalreserve.gov/BOARD DOCS/SPEECHES/2000/20000306.htm> (accessed 5 August 2003).

Haddad, Charles. "UPS vs. FedEx: Ground Wars." *BusinessWeek,* 21 May 2001, 64.

Hafner, Katie, and Matthew Lyon. *Where Wizards Stay Up Late: The Origins of the Internet.* New York: Simon & Schuster, 1996.

Hagel, John. *Out of the Box: Strategies for Achieving Profits Today and Growth Tomorrow Through Web Services.* Boston: Harvard Business School Press, 2002.

Hardy, Quentin. "We Did It." *Forbes,* 11 August 2003, 76.

Harvey, Fiona. "Michael Dell of Dell Computer." *Financial Times,* 5 August 2003.

Hayes, Brian. "The First Fifty Years." *CIO Insight,* 1 November 2001. <http://www.cioinsight.com/article2/0,3959,49331,00.asp> (accessed 12 June 2003).

Hildebrand, Carol. "Why Squirrels Manage Storage Better than You Do." *Darwin,* April 2003. <http://www.darwinmag.com/read/ 040102/squirrels.html> (accessed 10 January 2003).

Hitt, Lorin M., and Erik Brynjolfsson. "Productivity, Business Profitability, and Consumer Surplus: Three *Different* Measures of Information Technology Value." *MIS Quarterly* 20, no. 2 (June 1996): 121–142.

Hobsbawm, Eric. *The Age of Capital, 1848–1875.* New York: Vintage, 1996.

———. *The Age of Empire, 1875–1914.* New York: Vintage, 1989.

Hof, Robert D. "The Quest for the Next Big Thing." *BusinessWeek,* 18–25 August 2003, 92.

Hopper, Max D. "Rattling SABRE—New Ways to Compete on Information." *Harvard Business Review,* May-June 1990, 118–125.

Jones, Kathryn. "The Dell Way." *Business 2.0,* February 2003, 60.

Kaye, Doug. *LooselyCoupled: The Missing Pieces of Web Services.* Marin County, California: RDS Press, 2003.

Kharif, Olga. "The Fiber-Optic 'Glut'—in a New Light." *BusinessWeek Online,* 31 August 2001. <http://www.businessweek.com/bwdaily/dnflash/aug2001/nf20010831_396.htm> (accessed 18 December 2002).

Koch, Christopher. "The Battle for Web Services." *CIO,* 1 October 2003. <http://www.cio.com/archive/100103/standards.html> (accessed 25 November 2003).

———. "Your Open Source Plan." *CIO,* 15 March 2003, 58.

KPMG. "Project Risk Management: Information Risk Management." London: KPMG U.K., June 1999.

Landes, David S. *The Unbound Prometheus.* London: Cambridge University Press, 1969.

Landler, Mark. "Titans Still Gather at Davos, Shorn of Profits and Bavado." *New York Times,* 27 January 2003.

Lewis, William W., Vincent Palmade, Baudouin Regout, and Allen P. Webb, "What's Right with the U.S. Economy." *McKinsey Quarterly,* no. 1, 2002. <http://www.mckinseyquarterly.com/article_page.asp?L2=19&L3=67&ar=1151&pagenum=1> (accessed 23 August 2003).

Lohr, Steve. *Go To.* New York: Basic Books, 2001.

Lynch, Kevin. "Network Software: Finding the Perfect Fit." *Inbound Logistics,* November 2002. <http://www.inboundlogistics.com/articles/itmatters/itmatters1102.shtml> (accessed 8 July 2003).

Madan, Rajen, Carsten Sørenson, and Susan V. Scott. "'Strategy Sort of Died Around April of Last Year for a Lot of Us': CIO Perceptions on ICT Value and Strategy in the U.K. Financial Sector." Paper presented at the 11th European Conference on Information Systems, Naples, Italy, 19–21 June 2003.

Magretta, Joan, with Nan Stone. *What Management Is: How It Works and Why It's Everyone's Business.* New York: Free Press, 2002.

Malone, Thomas W. *The Future of Work: How the New Order of Business Will Shape Your Organization, Your Management Style and Your Life.* Boston: Harvard Business School Press, 2004.

Mangalindan, Mylene. "Oracle's Larry Ellison Expects Greater Innovation from Sector." *Wall Street Journal,* 8 April 2003.

Markoff, John, and Steve Lohr. "Intel's Huge Bet Turns Iffy." *New York Times,* 29 September 2002.

Marshall, Charles, Benn Konsynski, and John Sviokla. "Baxter International: OnCall as Soon as Possible?" Harvard Business School Case #9-195-103, 1994 (revised 29 March 1996).

McAfee, Andrew. "New Technologies, Old Organizational Forms? Reassessing the Impact of IT on Markets and Hierarchies." Harvard Business School Working Paper 03-078, April 2003.

McKenney, James L., with Duncan C. Copeland and Richard O. Mason. *Waves of Change: Business Evolution Through Information Technology.* Boston: Harvard Business School Press, 1995.

McKinsey Global Institute, "Whatever Happened to the New Economy?" Report of the McKinsey Global Institute, November 2002.

McNealy, Scott. Keynote speech at SunNetwork 2003 conference, San Francisco, 16 September 2003. <www.sun.com/aboutsun/media/presskits/networkcomputing03q3/mcnealykeynote.pdf> (accessed 1 October 2003).

Means, Grady. "Economics' New Dimensions: Why They're Extreme, Dramatic and Radical." Keynote address at Oracle AppsWorld 2001, New Orleans, 20–23 February 2001. <http://www.it-global forum.org/panamit/dscgi/ds.py/Get/File-1056/Page_45-58_Oracle_Bus_Report.pdf> (accessed 15 July 2003).

Micklethwait, John, and Adrian Wooldridge. *The Company: A Short History of a Revolutionary Idea.* New York: Modern Library, 2003.

Microsoft. "What .NET Means for IT Professionals." 24 July 2002.

<http://www.microsoft.com/net/business/it_pros.asp> (accessed 28 June 2003).

"Modifying Moore's Law." *The Economist,* Survey: The IT Industry, 10 May 2003, 5.

Moran, Nuala. "Looking for Savings on Distant Horizons." *Financial Times,* 2 July 2003.

"Moving Up the Stack." *The Economist,* Survey: The IT Industry, 10 May 2003, 6.

Negroponte, Nicholas. *Being Digital.* New York: Knopf, 1995.

Netcraft. "July 2003 Web Server Survey." <http://news.netcraft. com/archives/2003/07/02/july_2003_web_server_survey.html> (accessed 7 July 2003).

Newing, Rod, and Paul Strassman. "Watch the Economics and the Risk, Not the Technology." *Financial Times,* 5 December 2001.

Nonnenmacher, Tomas. "History of the U.S. Telegraph Industry." *EH.Net Encyclopedia of Economic and Business History.* 15 August 2001. <http://www.eh.net/encyclopedia/nonnenmacher.industry. telegraphic.us.php> (accessed 20 June 2003).

Nye, David E. *Electrifying America: Social Meanings of a New Technology.* Cambridge: MIT Press, 1990.

O'Farrell, Peter. "Carr Goes Off the Rail." Cutter Consortium Executive Update 4, no. 7, 2003. <http://www.cutter.com/freestuff/ bttu0307.html#ofarrell> accessed 4 October 2003).

Okin, Harvey, and Daniel Pfau. "Connecting Information Technology to the Business." *Accenture Outlook,* 2000.

Oliner, Stephen D., and Daniel E. Sichel. "The Resurgence of Growth in the Late 1990s: Is Information Technology the Story?" Federal Reserve Board white paper, February 2000. (Later published in *Journal of Economic Perspectives* 14, Fall 2000, 3–22.)

Park, Andrew, and Peter Burrows. "Dell, the Conqueror." *Business-Week,* 24 September 2001, 92.

Petzinger, Thomas Jr. *Hard Landing: The Epic Contest for Power and Profits That Plunged the Airlines into Chaos.* New York: Times Books, 1995.

Phillips, Tim. "The Bulletin Interview: Larry Ellison." *The Computer Bulletin,* July 2002. <http://www.bcs.org.uk/publicat/ebull/july02/ intervie.htm> (accessed 7 January 2003).

Pilat, Dirk, and Andrew Wyckoff, "The Impacts of ICT on Economic Performance—An International Comparison at Three Levels of Analysis." Paper presented at the U.S. Department of Commerce conference, Transforming Enterprise, January 2003.

Pohlmann, Tom, with Christopher Mines and Meredith Child. *Linking IT Spend to Business Results*. Forrester Research report, October 2002.

Porter, Michael E. *Competitive Advantage: Creating and Sustaining Superior Performance*. New York: Free Press, 1985.

———. "Strategy and the Internet." *Harvard Business Review,* March 2001, 62–78.

Prasad, Baba, and Patrick T. Harker. "Examining the Contribution of Information Technology Toward Productivity and Profitability in U.S. Retail Banking." Wharton Financial Institutions Center Working Paper 97-09, March 1997, 18.

Progressive Policy Institute. "Computer Costs Are Plummeting." *The New Economy Index,* November 1998. <http://www.neweconomy index.org/section1_page12.html> (accessed 12 January 2003).

Read, Donald. *The Power of News: The History of Reuters, 1849–1989*. Oxford: Oxford University Press, 1992.

Reimers, Barbara DePompa. "Five Cost-Cutting Strategies for Data Storage." *Computerworld,*21 October 2002. <http://www.computer world.com/hardwaretopics/storage/story/0,10801,75221,00.html> (accessed 5 February 2003).

Ricadela, Aaron. "Amazon Says It's Spending Less on IT." *Information Week,* 31 October 2001. <http://www.informationweek.com/story/IWK20011031S0005> (accessed 7 July 2003).

Ristelhueber, Robert, and Jennifer Baljko Shah. "Energy Crisis Threatens Silicon Valley's Growth." *EBN,* 19 January 2001. <http://www.ebnonline.com/story/OEG20010119S0033> (accessed 11 August 2003).

Roth, Daniel. "Can EMC Restore Its Glory?" *Fortune,* 8 July 2002, 107.

Schrage, Michael. "Wal-Mart Trumps Moore's Law." *Technology Review,* March 2002, 21.

Schurr, Sam H., Calvin C. Burwell, Warren D. Devine Jr., and Sidney Sonenblum. *Electricity in the American Economy: Agent of Technological Progress*. Westport, CT: Greenwood Press, 1990.

Shapiro, Carl, and Hal R. Varian. *Information Rules: A Strategic Guide to the Network Economy*. Boston: Harvard Business School Press, 1999.

Sliwa, Carol. "Wal-Mart Suppliers Shoulder Burden of Daunting RFID Effort." *Computerworld,* 10 November 2003. <http://www.computerworld.com/news/2003/story/0,11280,86978,00.html> (accessed 25 November 2003).

Slywotzky, Adrian, and Richard Wise. "An Unfinished Revolution." *MIT Sloan Management Review* 44, no. 3 (Spring 2003), 94.

Smith, Howard, and Peter Fingar. "21st Century Business Architecture." 2003. <http://www.bpmi.org/bpmi-library/D7B509F211.BPM21CArch.pdf> (accessed 29 September 2003.

Solow, Robert M. "We'd Better Watch Out." *New York Times Book Review,* 12 July 1987, 36.

Standage, Tom. *The Victorian Internet*. New York: Walker & Company, 1998.

Standish Group. "Chaos: A Recipe for Success." Report of the Standish Group, 1999.

———. "The Chaos Report (1994)." Report of the Standish Group, 1994.

Tapscott, Don. "Rethinking Strategy in a Networked World." *Strategy and Business,* no. 24, Third Quarter 2001, 39.

Tapscott, Don, David Ticoll, and Alex Lowy. *Digital Capital: Harnessing the Power of Business Webs*. Boston: Harvard Business School Press, 2000.

Taylor, Paul. "GE: Trailblazing the Indian Phenomenon." *Financial Times,* 2 July 2003.

Thurm, Scott, and Nick Wingfield. "How Titans Swallowed Wi-Fi, Stifling Silicon Valley Uprising." *Wall Street Journal,* 8 August 2003.

Ticoll, David. "In Writing Off IT, You Write Off Innovation." *Toronto Globe and Mail,* 29 May 2003.

U.S. Department of Commerce. *The Emerging Digital Economy*. April 1998.

Varian, Hal R. "If There Was a New Economy, Why Wasn't There a New Economics?" *New York Times,* 17 January 2002.

Veryard, Richard. *The Component-Based Business: Plug and Play*. London: Springer, 2000.

Walker, Rob. "Interview with Marcian (Ted) Hoff." *Silicon Genesis: Oral Histories of Semiconductor Industry Pioneers.* 3 March 1995. <http://www.stanford.edu/group/mmdd/SiliconValley/Silicon Genesis/TedHoff/Hoff.html> (accessed 16 June 2003).

Waters, Richard. "Corporate Computing Tries to Find a New Path." *Financial Times,* 4 June 2003.

————. "In Search of More for Less," *Financial Times,* 29 April 2003.

Weinstein, Bernard L., and Terry L. Clower. "The Impacts of the Union Pacific Service Disruptions on the Texas and National Economies: An Unfinished Story." Report prepared for the Railroad Commission of Texas by the University of North Texas Center for Economic Development and Research, 9 February 1998.

Welch, Jack, with John A. Byrne. *Jack: Straight from the Gut.* New York: Warner Books, 2001.

Zakon, Robert H'obbes'. "Hobbes' Internet Timeline v. 6.1." 2003. <http://www.zakon.org/robert/internet/timeline> (accessed 23 January 2003).

Zygmont, Jeffrey. *Microchip: An Idea, Its Genesis, and the Revolution It Created.* Cambridge, MA: Perseus, 2003.

The Great Debate: Responses to "IT Doesn't Matter"

My article "IT Doesn't Matter," published in the May 2003 issue of the *Harvard Business Review*, provoked many varied responses. Following are some of the most noteworthy, representing all sides of the issue. This selection is limited to articles and speeches in English. For a more comprehensive list, see www.nicholasgcarr.com/articles/matter.html.

Andrews, Paul. "IT Does Matter; Fixing It Might Just Convince Us." *Seattle Times,* 23 June 2003.

Boston, Brad. "Cisco Systems' CIO Brad Boston Responds to Nicholas G. Carr's Article 'IT Doesn't Matter.'" 25 June 2003. <http://newsroom.cisco.com/dlls/hd_062503.html> (accessed 26 June 2003).

Branscombe, Mary. "Fair Exchange." *The Guardian* (London), 12 June 2003.

Champy, James. "Technology Doesn't Matter—But Only at Harvard." *Fast Company,* December 2003, 119.

Colony, George F. "Low Icebergs." *Forrester.com,* 17 June 2003. <http://www.forrester.com/ER/Research/Brief/0,1317,16990,00.html> (accessed 20 October 2003).

Comper, Tony. "Back to the Future: A CEO's Perspective on the IT Post-Revolution." Speech at the IBM Global Financial Services Forum, San Francisco, 8 September 2003. <http://www2.bmo.com/speech/article/0,1259,contentCode-3294_divId-4_langId-1_navCode-124,00.html> (accessed 23 September 2003).

"Does IT Matter? An HBR Debate," *Harvard Business Review,* June 2003, <harvardbusinessonline.hbsp.harvard.edu/b01/en/files/topic/Web_Letters.pdf> (accessed 3 July 2003). This electronic document collects letters written to the editor of the *Harvard Business Review* by John Seely Brown and John Hagel III, F. Warren McFarlan and Richard L. Nolan, Paul A. Strassman, Vladimir Zwass, and Vijay Gurbaxani, among others, and includes an introduction by Thomas A. Stewart and a response from me.

Evans, Bob. "IT Doesn't Matter?" *Information Week,* 12 May 2003. <http://www.informationweek.com/story/showArticle.jhtml?articleID=9800088> (accessed 15 May 2003).

———. "IT Is a Must, No Matter How You View It." *Information Week,* 19 May 2003. <http://www.informationweek.com/story/showArticle.jhtml?articleID=10000185> (accessed 28 May 2003).

Farber, Dan. "The End of IT as We Know It?" *ZDNet,* 28 May 2003. <http://techupdate.zdnet.com/techupdate/stories/main/0,14179,2913824,00.html> (accessed 5 June 2003).

———. "What Matters More Than IT." *ZDNet,* 30 September 2003.
<http://techupdate.zdnet.com/techupdate/stories/main/0,14179,2914761,00.html> (accessed 8 October 2003).

Gates, Bill. Remarks at the Microsoft CEO Summit. Redmond, Washington, 21 May 2003. <http://www.microsoft.com/billgates/speeches/2003/05-21ceosummit2003.asp> (accessed 4 June 2003).

Hayes, Frank. "IT Delivers." *Computerworld,* 19 May 2003. <http://www.computerworld.com/managementtopics/management/story/0,10801,81278,00.html> (accessed 1 June 2003).

Hof, Robert D. "Andy Grove: 'We Can't Even Glimpse the Potential.'" *BusinessWeek,* 25 August 2003, 86.

———. "Nick Carr: The Tech Advantage Is Overrated." *Business-Week,* 25 August 2003, 82.

Keefe, Patricia. "IT Does Matter." *Computerworld,* 12 May 2003. <http://www.computerworld.com/managementtopics/management/story/0,10801,81094,00.html> (accessed 15 May 2003).

Kirkpatrick, David. "Does IT Matter? CEOs and CIOs Sound Off." *Fortune,* 3 June 2003. < http://www.fortune.com/fortune/fastforward/0,15704,456246,00.html> (accessed 5 June 2003).

———. "Stupid-Journal Alert." *Fortune,* 27 May 2003. <http://www.fortune.com/fortune/fastforward/0,15704,454727,00.html> (accessed 5 June 2003).

Langberg, Mike. "IT's Future: Invisible or Invaluable?" *San Jose Mercury News,* 16 June 2003.

Lashinsky, Adam. "Tech Matters. So What?" *CNN Money,* 28 May 2003. <http://money.cnn.com/2003/05/27/commentary/bottomline/lashinsky/> (accessed 5 June 2003).

Leibs, Scott. "An Exercise in Utility." *CFO.com,* 16 June 2003. <http://www.cfo.com/article/1,5309,9743%7C%7CM%7C606,00.html> (accessed 18 June 2003).

Levy, Steven. "Twilight of the PC Era?" *Newsweek,* 24 November 2003, 54.

Lohr, Steve. "A New Technology, Now That New Is Old." *New York Times,* 4 May 2003.

———. "Has Technology Lost Its 'Special' Status?" *New York Times,* 16 May 2003.

Maney, Kevin. "How IBM, Dell Managed to Build Crushing Tech Dominance." *USA Today,* 20 May 2003.

Melymuka, Kathleen. "Get Over Yourself" (interview with Nicholas G. Carr). *Computerworld,* 12 May 2003. <http://www.computerworld.com/managementtopics/roi/story/0,10801,81045,00.html> (accessed 15 May 2003).

———. "IT Does So Matter!" (interview with Rob Austin, Andrew McAfee, Paul Strassman, and Tom DeMarco). *Computerworld,* 7 July 2003. <http://www.computerworld.com/managementtopics/roi/story/0,10801,82738,00.html> (accessed 12 July 2003).

Mendham, Tim. "Fightin' Words." *CIO Australia,* 8 October 2003. <http://www.cio.com.au/index.php?id=1599085755&fp=16& fpid=0> (accessed 11 October 2003).

Morris, James A. "IT Still It—in Essential, Enabling Sort of Way." *Pittsburgh Post-Gazette,* 7 September 2003.

Schrage, Michael. "Why IT Really Does Matter." *CIO,* 1 August 2003. <http://www.cio.com/archive/080103/work.html> (accessed 3 August 2003).

Smith, Howard, and Peter Fingar. *IT Doesn't Matter—Business Processes Do: A Critical Analysis of Nicholas Carr's I.T. Article in the* Harvard Business Review. Tampa: Meghan-Kiffer, 2003.

Steinke, Steve. "IT? Does It Matter?" *NetworkMagazine.com,* 7 July 2003. <http://www.networkmagazine.com/shared/article/show Article.jhtml?articleId=10818275&classroom=> (accessed 22 July 2003).

Taschek, John. "IT Does Matter." *Eweek,* 14 July 2003. <http:// www.eweek.com/article2/0,3959,1192040,00.asp> (accessed 21 July 2003).

Vaas, Lisa. "IT Losing Steam?" *Eweek,* 2 June 2003. <http://www. eweek.com/article2/0,3959,1115053,00.asp> (accessed 10 June 2003).

Walker, Leslie. "Falling Off of the Cutting Edge." *Washington Post,* 29 May 2003.

Weisman, Robert. "Tech-as-Commodity Debate Will Be Spring Rage." *Boston Globe,* 3 August 2003.

Index

About the Author

NICHOLAS G. CARR is an independent business writer whose work centers on business strategy, information technology, and their intersection. He has written more than a dozen articles and interviews for the *Harvard Business Review,* including "IT Doesn't Matter," "Hypermediation: Commerce as Clickstream," and "Being Virtual: Character and the New Economy." He has also written for the *Financial Times,* the *Boston Globe,* and *Business 2.0* and was a columnist for the *Industry Standard* for more than a year.

Between 1997 and 2003, Carr held top editorial positions at the *Harvard Business Review,* including executive editor and, for most of 2002, acting editor. Articles he edited won McKinsey Awards as the best articles published in *HBR* in 1999, 2000, 2001, and 2002. Before joining *HBR,* he was a principal at Mercer Management Consulting.

Carr has been a featured speaker at many business events, including the Harvard Internet & Society Conference, the Harvard Business School Strategy and the Business Environment Conference, Comdex, the Government CIO Summit, and the Forbes/IBM Executive Forum. His ideas have been featured in the *New York Times, BusinessWeek, Forbes, Fortune, Fast Company,* the *Washington Post,* and *CIO,* among other publications. He holds a B.A. from Dartmouth College and an M.A. from Harvard University.

More information on Carr and his work can be found at www.nicholasgcarr.com.